WAR LORD

WAR LORD

KHALIFA HAFTAR AND THE FUTURE OF LIBYA

John Oakes

AMBERLEY

To *June* in memoriam

and

To Nikki and Becky

First published 2021

Amberley Publishing
The Hill, Stroud
Gloucestershire, GL5 4EP

www.amberley-books.com

Copyright © John Oakes, 2021

The right of John Oakes to be identified as
the Author of this work has been asserted in
accordance with the Copyright, Designs and
Patents Act 1988.

ISBN 978 1 3981 0778 6 (hardback)
ISBN 978 1 3981 0779 3 (ebook)

British Library Cataloguing in Publication Data.
A catalogue record for this book is available
from the British Library.

1 2 3 4 5 6 7 8 9 10

Typesetting by SJmagic DESIGN SERVICES, India.
Printed in the UK.

CONTENTS

Preface   7

Maps   10

Introduction   13

Prologue: The Long Road from Ouadi Doum   19

1 Haftar's World   21

2 Officers, Gentlemen and Plotters   34

3 King Idris and a Changing Libya   63

4 Haftar in the Heart of Darkness   91

5 Arab Spring or Winter of Discontent?   116

6 Democracy or Theocracy?   143

7 Can Haftar Survive?   171

8 Haftar Returns to Libya   198

9 End Game?   221

Afterword   243

Select Bibliography   259

Acknowledgements   261

Index   263

PREFACE

I was posted to Libya in 1958 and remained there for more than eight years, roughly four of which were spent in Tripoli and four in Benghazi. The nature of my work meant that I travelled widely and often throughout the country, which was then in a state of transition and struggling to adapt to recently won independence and the discovery of large oil reserves. My wife worked for an oil exploration company in Tripoli and shared with me stories of her work and the company of her friends. Between us we learned much about the impact of the modern world on one of its poorest nations. My duties prevented me from carrying out all but the briefest of academic enquiries at the time, but my contacts with the Libyan people and their country enabled me to read the literature which forms the basis of this book in the light of my own experience.

The great changes in Libyan society caused by independence in 1951 and by the discovery of oil in 1961 were beginning to take place. The economy, hitherto dependent on Italian colonists, and latterly British and US military bases, was beginning to feel the effect of growing oil revenue. The lack of technical, bureaucratic, financial and commercial expertise was acute. The infrastructure was inadequate. Migration from the hinterlands to the two cities, Tripoli and Benghazi, was accelerating and improvised dwellings made from corrugated iron at best or wood and cardboard at worst were growing on the city fringes.

Regional differences were still strong and enhanced by history and geography. The concept of Libya as an independent and unified state was new. Much power was vested in its king, who was ageing and temperamentally unsuited to governing the transition from one of the poorest countries in the world into an oil-rich nation.

In 2011 I began to write and blog about Libya. My blog charted the implosion of Libya following the demise of Ghaddafi and reflects my research and interpretation of that turbulent time. It has gained a worldwide readership which sometimes surprises and often encourages me to believe that interest in Libya's manifold troubles remains strong.

Throughout the period covered by my blog there appeared a number of key personalities, the most prominent of which was Field Marshal Khalifa Haftar. He has been called a war lord and a self-styled field marshal by his enemies and this has been echoed by the international media. Yet in my view – and in the view of many others – he has become the one person who holds the key to Libya's future. I have, therefore, used his life and times as a clothesline on which to hang the story of Libya's collapse into civil war and its possible emergence into relative peace.

As to history, I have said little in this book about the Greek, Roman and Byzantine occupation of Libya. I have attached much importance but few words to the Hilalian invasion of Libya in the mid-eleventh century and I have written a little about the Ottoman period but only in so far as it is relevant to the present proxy war in Libya. The Italian colonisation and rule had a significant effect on Libya today, and the involvement of France in Libya's south and its watchfulness over Chad, Niger and Tunisia has prompted some longer excursions into their recent history and present policy in the region.

There are a few brief stories from my own life in Libya interspersed among the narratives. I have tried not to intrude on the reader's patience too much. Garrulous geriatrics can test the good manners of even the most patient. However, if you are to understand the conditions on the people-trafficking routes or the life of a displaced family in Libya today it is useful to know what it is like to endure a sandstorm, wade through a wadi in the rainy season, survive a protracted interrogation or rely on a doubtful motor vehicle in a desert.

There is a notable omission in most of the writing about Libya: the voice and views of women. I have not been able to fill this void except for the few brief stories my wife told me about the cloistered life of women in Tripoli in the last century. Only in the work of Emrys Peters is there much to be found about Bedouin women, and I suspect he too was indebted to his wife for the rare insights he has given us as she accompanied him during his research in the field. It seemed that the Arab Spring would encourage the emergence of women in politics and journalism until a leading voice of Libyan feminism was silenced by a bullet in the awful period of targeted killings in Benghazi.

There is the matter of transliterating Arabic words and place names into English to account for. I have chosen the easiest version and tried to be consistent. I confess to a sentimental attachment to an older spelling of some place names.

In the matter of sources. This book is based on the conversations I had with Libyan colleagues and the records I made during the eight years or more I lived and worked in Libya, the research I carried out for my book about Libya in 2011 and the blog I have been writing since 2011 which can be found at Libyastories.com. I have harvested much from the blog and my personal records, and the reader will do well to take that into account when weighing the value of my assertions and opinions. They might well suffer from the sin of subjectivity.

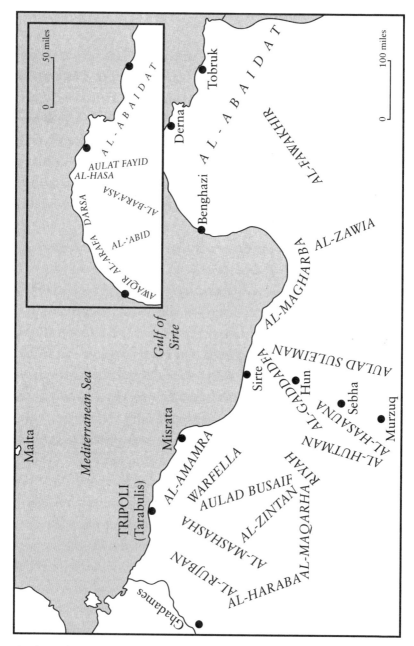

Arab and Arab Berber tribes of Libya

A map showing many of Libya's Arab and Arab Berber tribal homelands. The Amazigh, Tuareg and Tebu homelands are not shown but are in the north-west, south-west and south-east respectively. This map is compiled from those made by Colonel di Agostini and his staff during the Italian occupation of Libya. No survey of the tribes has been published since.

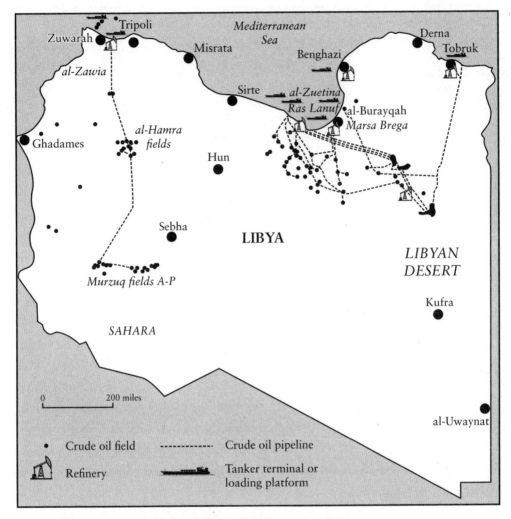

Map of crude oil pipelines and oil ports of Libya
This map shows the distribution of Libya's crude oil pipelines, oil ports and refineries and how difficult they are to defend. More fields may come into production if a peaceful solution to Libya's troubles emerges.

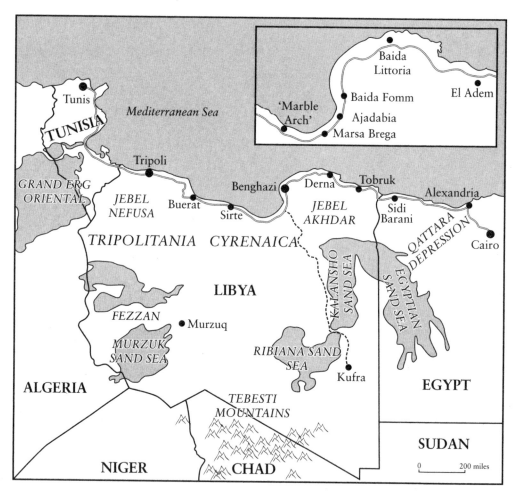

Map of Libya
Libya as it was in Khalifa Haftar's childhood and early youth,
showing the main geographical features such as sand seas and
mountainous regions. The three provinces are named Cyrenaica,
Tripolitania and the Fezzan. They have recently been known as
East, West and South Libya, but the old provincial names are
re-emerging.

INTRODUCTION

Since the Arab Spring and anti-Ghaddafi uprising on the streets of Benghazi on 14 February 2011, Libyans have known little or no rest from violence. In the vacuum left by the demise of Muammar Ghaddafi, power shifted substantially into the hands of local war lords, tribal elders and jihadist militia leaders. The crucial failure to either disband the militias raised to fight Ghaddafi or assimilate them into the army left them armed and dangerous. In Benghazi, Derna and Sirte militant Islamists took control and exercised power with notable brutality. In Sebha, intertribal strife reached intolerable levels. In Tripoli and Misrata, armed militias held sway.

In June 2014 an attempt to settle Libya's political leadership by means of a democratic election was played out – in a heatwave and under the threat of armed conflict. For a time, Libya had two governments and targeted killings became frequent. On 25 June, the feminist lawyer Salwa Bughaighis was shot dead in her own home by four assassins. Her death received little attention – either in Libya or abroad – but it was highly symbolic of the divisions which still threaten to tear Libya and much of the Islamic world apart.

Khalifa Haftar's forces were aligned against the Islamist militias, and there followed a surge of violence which both accelerated and widened. A political solution seemed impossible, so an intense international effort to reach a peaceful settlement commenced. Eventually, the United Nations brokered a Libyan Political Agreement which gained the recognition of the UN General Assembly and formed a Government of National Accord (GNA). It met for the first time in Tunis on 8 January 2016 and was later inserted into Tripoli, taking possession of the offices of government by 30 March 2016.

The disparate groups left over from the fall of Ghaddafi, together with units of the regular army, now largely coalesced into two major entities: those that aligned themselves with Field Marshal Khalifa Haftar's Libyan National Army on one side, and those that supported the GNA on the other.

Despite being the internationally recognised government of Libya, the GNA has been unable to assert control within Tripoli and in wider Libya. It is functioning ineffectively without a popular mandate and has recently allied itself with President Erdogan of Turkey.

On the other side, Khalifa Haftar has gained support – and not just from within Libya. He not only has the backing of the United Arab Emirates and guarded but active support from Egypt and the Sahel countries, but Germany and France have afforded him a high-profile welcome. Even Putin continues to turn a blind eye to a well-connected and highly trained Russian mercenary group that is fighting alongside Haftar's Libyan National Army.

How has a relatively unknown renegade commander garnered so much international support? The answer may lie in the fear engendered by Islamic Jihadists finding refuge and wielding influence in Tripoli and Misrata, or in the constant stream of economic migrants and refugees on the trans-Saharan people-trafficking routes. Or possibly from the well-corroborated evidence of corruption emerging from Tripoli. Haftar has strengthened his military presence in the south of Libya with the intention of discouraging people trafficking and dissident groups from the Sahel countries in which the French show a deal of interest. Haftar's control over Libya's oil industry is a considerable asset in his diplomatic negotiations. The possibility that he might win makes him an attractive wager.

Meanwhile, President Erdogan is advancing his expansionist ambitions, probably to secure his domestic position but certainly to gain access to the natural gas reserves in the Eastern Mediterranean. In this regard he is at odds with Greece, Cyprus, Egypt and others who have a stake in the gas field and claim that Turkey does not. Erdogan has entered into a treaty with the Tripoli Government of National Accord which allows him to blister onto Libya's rightful access. He is also allied to the Muslim Brotherhood, which has been outlawed by Egypt and causes concern in other Arab countries. Turkey itself is sharply divided between the supporters of Political Islam and the Secularists, a divide which is now also evident in Libya.

As a consequence of these alliances, a proxy war has developed in Libya between Turkey on one side and the United Arab Emirates and Egypt on the other. Turkey is supplying homemade drones and Syrian militias to Haftar's enemies, and its intervention supports the forces of political Islam against Haftar's more secular allies. Some sources suggest that Turkey has established logistical bases in neighbouring Tunis so as to circumvent international monitoring of the Libyan arms embargo. Meanwhile, the UAE equips Haftar with Chinese drones and hi-tech military hardware. Putin has decided Haftar may be the likely winner but is hedging his bets.

Inside Libya, that Haftar holds the ace cards is in no doubt. On 17 October 2017 he told a meeting of his army commanders in Benghazi that the size of Libya is 1,760,000 square kilometres and that his Libyan National Army controls all but 30,000 square kilometres of it. But projecting military power in such a huge country is not easy. The terrain is notably inhospitable, there are limits to the range of even modern war planes, and logistics are a nightmare. Even once you have won it, defending such a large territory is nigh on impossible. So how does Haftar do it?

Haftar's strength is not in operational military leadership. He has cobbled together widely separate ethnic and religious factions into a functioning army. He has insisted on training his troops as well as possible. He delegates well and has a good chief of staff. He has demonstrated timing, a grasp of history, good public relations, propaganda skills, an understanding of public opinion and, it must be said, decisive ruthlessness.

Haftar also has a perception of the unique nature of Libyan tribes. Around the time of the Norman conquest and subjugation of England, two belligerent Arab tribes from the Nejd migrated through Egypt into Libya. They drove many of the Berber tribes from their homelands and assumed ownership by right of conquest. The seven major tribes of East Libya and many tribes in the south and west of Libya assert that their origin derives directly from their invading Arab ancestors. Berber tribes found shelter in the mountains in the west and some Berbers remained and intermarried with their Arab conquerors to form mixed tribes. Many of the latter tribes live as clients within or alongside the Arabs and some are unchallenged masters of their own territory.

Haftar is not a typical military leader, but then the war he is fighting is not a typical war. The situation in Libya is a crucible of tribal loyalties, religious fervour, ethnic differences, personal animosities, unresolved disputes, access to great oil reserves and international tensions. Haftar's war is testing the advances in modern warfare. He is using highly mobile Operation Rooms which facilitate and accelerate decision making from skirmish to theatre level and encourage military creativity, but also allow him unprecedented control. He, and his enemies, are using new and better drones and precision artillery. We cannot escape the interesting and growing importance in warfare of social media, sophisticated and targeted propaganda and of data analysis. Haftar's war is not just a storm in the desert but a lesson for those interested in urban warfare and proxy wars and even for those who would intervene in the affairs of other nations without due diligence.

Libya's civil wars have demonstrated a disconcerting paradox. It is now possible for acts of violence to be recorded on modern mobile phones and broadcast on local TV channels and social media in order to intimidate opponents or strike fear among civilians. The absence of trusted international news correspondents means that an escalation of brutality would escape a wider, more discerning audience. Violence begets violence and both sides tend towards a parity of menace. Haftar is likely to have made what we might call necessary allies who may implicate him by committing atrocities he will find hard to justify. How does he measure up against this yardstick?

The accepted doctrine is that success in civil war is achieved by strong leadership, ruthless tactics, effective propaganda and geographical positioning. Does Haftar possess the energy, organising ability, charisma and drive to see his self-appointed task through to a conclusion?

This book is not a biography of Khalifa Haftar. It doesn't explore more than the bare bones of his personal life other than his background and upbringing. It is not an exploration of the man or a chronology of his life. But for the student of modern warfare, Haftar gives an opportunity to discover much – not only about Libya, or about military control, but about the nature of the human condition. Haftar is perhaps one of the most experienced military leaders in the world today. He is also one of the most divisive. Watching the unfolding events in this unstable region through the lens of his life affords us unprecedented insight into the past, and a grasp of what the future could hold for Libya and its people.

Prologue

THE LONG ROAD FROM OUADI DOUM

It was an audacious move. On 19 February 2020, Field Marshal Khalifa Haftar, the overall commander of the Libyan National Army, announced that the country's oil fields and terminals had been shut down. Confirming the announcement was Libya's National Oil Corporation, which told the press shortly afterwards that oil production had dropped to just 191,475 barrels per day – a loss of over $1.3 billion.

Libya is totally dependent on the rich and bountiful oil fields deep in its desert hinterland. Oil is by far its main source of income. Cutting off the lifeblood of the country was a dramatic demonstration of Haftar's power at a time when the United Nations was attempting to broker a lasting ceasefire and an end to the civil war that has crippled the already damaged country for decades.

How did he do it? Did his army storm the oil terminals, firing wildly with their AK47s from the backs of their careering camels? Not so, though it would have made a dramatic story. No, the most dramatic aspect of this strangling of Libya's lifeblood is that it was done without force. Haftar's shutdown was made possible because, by some inexplicable force, this self-styled strongman has gained control over much of Libya. He has positioned himself at the gates of Tripoli, behind which his enemies are bottled up and seeking help. He has also waged a long and careful negotiation with the tribal sheiks, the powerful social clans who control much of the oil-rich areas of Libya. The result is their vocal and respected support. On 19 February, all Haftar had to do was simply tell the petroleum facilities guards to lock the gates and take the keys home.

At a moment such as this it might have occurred to Haftar that he was a long way from Ouadi Doum, the Libyan stronghold in northern Chad where his erstwhile and perfidious friend Colonel Muammar Ghaddafi had left him to rot over thirty years previously. His enemies, of which there is no shortage, would agree.

A successful attack on the Libyan airfield at Ouadi Doum in March 1987 had resulted not only in the capture of a stash of armed vehicles and aircraft but the death of Haftar's second-in-command. Haftar, along with numerous of his troops, was made a prisoner of war. He would have had a lot to think about in his Chadian prison, among which would be his abandonment – he might say betrayal – by Ghaddafi. Perhaps Haftar's actions are a partial vindication for his betrayal, an expression of his appetite for revenge, or an atonement for the dead. We cannot know for sure, and he would be unlikely to tell us. One thing is certain: no solution to Libya's manifold problems is now possible without the cooperation of Khalifa Haftar.

I

HAFTAR'S WORLD

In 1961 I was posted to Benghazi from Tripoli, where I had been stationed as an RAF officer. My predecessor had been highly qualified but undiplomatic – he had been hastily removed for punching a Libyan policeman who had offered him persistent and gratuitous advice. I was young and inexperienced. There were no others competing for the job.

I found Benghazi ramshackle and with war damage still in evidence. On the walls of the old Italian roadside waystations there still remained the graffiti left by British troops as they advanced and retreated in the battles of the Second World War. The lugubrious Kilroy, favourite graffiti cartoon character of the British soldiers, drooped his nose over a wall and declared that he was, in fact, here. The words 'you will not laugh as Gerry strafes – keep your head down' continued to exhort the peacetime traveller from numerous roadside walls. On the approach road to Tobruk a number of stones had been sculpted by a stonemason with the badges of the British Army units involved in the siege of Tobruk in 1941.

These were the benign artifacts of war. Not so long gone was most, but not all, of the damage to the vital infrastructure left by the war. I had an office in a hangar at Benina airport which had doors riddled with bullet holes. Benghazi had been bombed extensively, especially the port and docks, and Tobruk was also heavily damaged. Roads, bridges, telephone lines, dwellings and more were wrecked.

I was one of a few Englishmen still in Benghazi, still maintaining standards and hoping to be on the list of those invited to the annual British embassy garden party. After the Italian colonists had left Cyrenaica, Libya's eastern province, in 1942, Britain's role in the negotiations leading up to Libya's independence had been crucial, but for some years the British had been a pale shadow of their former selves in Libya. The Suez crisis had shown that Britain was no longer resolute and the old empire was folding up fast. The Americans were piling in. Drillers and riggers abounded and the accents of Texas, Louisiana and New Mexico replaced those of the Berks and Bucks.

Around 150km south of Benghazi was the town of Ajdabiya. I would stop there on my regular journeys from Benghazi to the developing oil ports on the shores of the Gulf of Sirte, eating a late breakfast in one of its cafes of a boiled egg and the strong, sweet coffee known in Libya as 'Ghid Ghid'. Groups of Bedouin tents could be seen some way out of town.

It was in Ajdabiya on 7 November 1943 that Khalifa Haftar was born. The winter of 1942/43 had been unusually rainy and General Erwin Rommel had been defeated at el Alamein. In retreat he was pursued by Montgomery's 8th Army and somewhat hampered by mud. He paused briefly at Ajdabiya, where there were two airfields which he used to resupply his diminished force before retreating behind Marsa Brega. Here the terrain creates a bottleneck which was easier to defend and allowed him to regroup. Despite the opposition of Hitler and Mussolini, who was frantically watching his colonial ambitions collapse, Rommel conducted an orderly retreat westward, where he would eventually stand to fight again in Tunisia. Mussolini's worst nightmare came true and his colony in Cyrenaica collapsed.

So rapidly did the Italian farmers evacuate their homes that some left the remains of lunch on their kitchen tables.

Ajdabiya is not only historically but politically significant. Despite the Italians' defeat by the British and Allies and their subsequent retreat, at the time of Khalifa Haftar's birth Libya was still officially a colonial possession of Italy.

Libya had been part of the Ottoman Empire from 1551 until 1911. The Italians had been interested in joining the scramble for Africa and had landed an army on the shores of Libya in 1911. They had beaten the resistance offered by the incumbent Turks and their Libyan allies and established colonies in the Mediterranean littoral before attempting to move inland by force of arms, invading the provinces of Cyrenaica in the east and Tripolitania in the west. They met with resistance in the hinterland, especially in Cyrenaica, where tribal irregulars took up arms against them.

But the Italian conquest of Libya began to take a more aggressive character when Benito Mussolini and his Fascist movement came to power in 1922. Mussolini's hold on the Italian working class was at first tenuous and he embarked on foreign adventures in the Horn of Africa and Libya to strengthen his domestic dominance. In both the Horn of Africa and Libya Mussolini's colonial policies were pursued with criminal brutality.

By now newly motivated and with aircraft in support, the Italians commenced the pacification of Libya in March 1923 with an attack by mechanised troops across the Barqa al-Hamra (the Red Plain) and the Barqa al-Baida (the White Plain), that is the western lands of the al-Awaquir tribe and the homeland of the al-Magharba and Zawiya tribes. Their objective was to seize Ajdabiya.

They besieged the town on 21 April. It was an easy victory over the ill-equipped Arab forces and the Italians expected their early capitulation. They later detached two mechanised columns to attack Marsa Brega in the west, but they were severely mauled by Magharba tribesmen. The terrain in this part of Libya is rough and consists mainly of dunes, and it would have been all too easy for the al-Magharba irregulars to raid and disconcert town-bred troops plodding through the sand.

The Italians learnt quickly that disciplined columns of troops moving in deliberate formation towards an objective were vulnerable to harassing attacks by Bedouin bands fighting in their homeland. They adopted a new strategy. They took to sending out flying columns of mechanised troops to raid the Bedouin camps, killing men, women and children without mercy, destroying the grain stores and flocks and then withdrawing quickly into their defended base in Ajdabiya. These terror raids were designed to kill as many Bedouin as possible.

In winter, when the camps were dispersed and the terrain impassable, the Italians took to flying over them and machine gunning indiscriminately. Stories of the awful strafing raids were still current when I was travelling about in Libya, and I heard first-hand of rebels being thrown alive out of aircraft onto their tribal camps. There are no official head counts, but the Italian census shows that the population of Cyrenaica dropped from 225,000 to 142,000 between 1928 and 1931. The number of sheep and goats on which the nomadic and semi-nomadic tribes depended dropped from 270,000 in 1930 to just 67,000 a year later.

The perpetrator of many of these raids was General Rodolfo Graziani, Vice Governor of Libya between 1930 and 1934. The most ruthlessly efficient of Italian proconsuls, he had arrived in Benghazi on 27 March 1930 when a Libyan tribal rebellion against the Italian occupation was at its height. He used a combination of arrest, restriction of civilian movement, strafing of recalcitrant tribes, public executions and concentration camps to subdue the rebels. Italian army units augmented by Christian

Eritrean soldiers blocked and poisoned desert wells, confiscated livestock and restricted seasonal migrations. Graziani's execution of the acknowledged leader of the rebels, the Senussi Sheik Omar al-Mukhtar, on 16 September 1931 before a captive audience of rebel prisoners was said to mark the beginning of the end of the rebellion. The guerrilla war against the Italians represents an historic struggle for independence in the minds of the Libyan people even today. Omar al-Mukhtar became their first national hero.

Mussolini framed his policy in Libya as the restoration of the Roman Empire. Here is General Graziani addressing a cohort of adolescent sons of Italian settlers from a balcony in Benghazi. They had just received their rifles in a ceremony marking their elevation to warrior status:

> Boys – today you received your rifles, the rifles you are going to use in the defence of Italy which we all love and for the furtherance of her honour if this is needed. Remember that in whatever you're doing that you are Italians, Romans, and remember your forebears were in this country. You are Romans fighting against barbarians. Be kind to them, but always be their superiors. Remember that you are Romans!

Mussolini declared war on the British on 10 June 1940 and moved his 10th Army from Libya into Egypt on 13 September. He did so despite the protests of General Graziani, whose military assessment of the possible outcome differed from his. The Italian leader was gambling on the imminent defeat of the British by Hitler's Germany. It appeared to him, as it probably did to many, that the Germans would win the Battle of Britain, launch Operation Sea Lion, occupy Britain and decapitate the British Empire. He would then be in a position to replace the defeated British in Egypt. The outcome was very different. His 10th Army was defeated in the Western Desert by a better-armed and more determined British army.

On 23 January 1943 Bernard Montgomery took the surrender of Tripoli and Rommel withdrew his forces to Tunisia. By February, the last German and Italian soldiers had been driven from Libya. On 3 September, with US and British forces threatening Rome, the Armistice of Cassible signed between the Italians and the Allies marked the end of Mussolini's belligerent gamble and the participation of Italy in the Second World War. The Italians were gone and the Allied occupation of Libya had begun.

In the two provinces, Cyrenaica in the east and Tripolitania in the west, a British Military Administration (BMA) took power on a 'care and maintenance' basis. In Libya's third province, the Fezzan in the south-west, the Free French set up a similar administration after General Le Clerc had loosened the Italian army's tenuous grip there.

The British Military Administration drew its leadership and advice from the Sudan Political Service, which was noted for selecting its personnel from high-flying graduates of the Universities of Oxford and Cambridge. One of these was Duncan Cumming, the first leader of the BMA. Educated at Giggleswick School and Gonville and Caius College, Cambridge, he was recruited into the Sudan Political Service, learned Arabic and gained an enviable reputation. The Second World War saw him first in Eritrea, where he set up a Military Administration in 1941 after the British had ejected the Italian colonists, so he was clearly well qualified to become the Chief Administrator of the newly formed BMA.

Cumming found Cyrenaica in a distressed state. The result of a decade of armed resistance to and draconian reprisals from the Italian colonialists was evident, not least from the attempt to settle Italian farmers in the fertile tribal lands of the Green Mountains. The semi-nomadic Libyan tribes in whose homelands they had been planted had no experience in Mediterranean agriculture, so the Italian farmsteads up on the Barce Plain were now unoccupied. The BMA attempted to make up for the acute food shortage in 1942/43 by bringing the land back into cultivation, but by the time I was there in the early 1960s it had reverted to pasture. I found the sad, small white dwellings, previously the homes of Italian farmers, occupied by animals, while the tribes lived in their accustomed tents.

In the south-west, the Fezzan, administered by the Free French, was ever different. Theirs was a military government, whereas the BMA was led by civilians, only in military uniform out of convenience and necessity. The French relied heavily on the Awlad Suleiman tribe to run the province. Claiming descent from the Beni Sulaim Arab invaders, as do the other Sa'adi tribes of Libya, its homeland stretched from the shores of the Gulf of Sirte to Sebha where it had rights to date palms. The progeny of its leader, Saif al-Nasr, are still respected today.

So, until Haftar's birth in 1942, the Libyans, especially in Cyrenaica, had lived under the yoke of colonial powers. They were largely excluded from government and education. They met modern civilisation with very few educated leaders, artisans, engineers, lawyers or even doctors. The legacies of war remained, and the scars of conflict would have been a common sight to the young Haftar and his contemporaries as they moved about the roads in Libya.

The town of Haftar's birth was significant in the Italian occupation largely because of geography. It forms something of a crossroads in northern Libya and is where the coastal road from Tripoli branches in three directions. The first goes north-east across the White and Red plains to Benghazi, while a second takes the hazardous route south-south-east in the direction of

Kufra and, eventually, as far south as the Jebal Uweinat. A third strikes out eastwards, roughly following the old Trig al-Abd camel track to Tobruk across the southern foothills of the Jebel Akhdar.

The Jebel Akhdar is a fertile, mountainous region, and it's not hard to see why it was attractive to the pure Bedouin Arabs of the Beni Hilal and the Beni Sulaim who migrated into Libya in the early part of the eleventh century. Sa'ada of the Beni Sulaim, their ancestress, gave her name to the nine Sa'adi tribes that resulted. These are the most prominent tribes in Libya and still sit at the top of the tribal hierarchy today. Other groups, known as the Marabtin tribes, live among the Sa'adi tribes as 'clients' and once paid them for the use of wells, soil and protection.

The tribes of Libya traditionally own their homeland collectively and by right of conquest and they are just as influential today as they have been for hundreds of years. For example, the al-Magharba tribe are the rightful owners of a long east-west homeland that stretches from the eastern boundary of the Ghaddadfa and the Awlad Suleman tribal homelands around the south-eastern shores of the Gulf of Sirte until it adjoins that of the al-Awaquir and al-Fawaqir tribes. In the past the al-Magharba had great skill in trading and their business contacts existed as far south as Kano in northern Nigeria. It is the al-Magharba tribe's dominance of the south-eastern shore of the Gulf of Sirte which gives them a hold over Libya's oil crescent today.

The al-Zawiya, known more often as the Zwai, spreads from Ajdabiya across vast interior regions that now contain major oil deposits and water sources. Desert traders and nomadic pastoralists, the al-Zawiya conquered Kufra in 1840, subduing the indigenous Tebu which had, at some time in antiquity, maintained a notable presence there. The Zawiya leadership promised the head of the Senussi sect, Mohamed

Ben Ali as-Senussi, a liberal donation of dates and water if he would establish a religious community there. This he did, and the Senussi order eventually moved its headquarters to Kufra. From here it exercised its moral and temporal suasion and commercial competence over the hitherto predatory al-Zawiya, establishing a profitable trade in slaves and arms between the south and the north until the Italians drove it out in 1931. Since that time, the al-Zawiya tribe has owned most of the date palm groves of the Kufra oases, employing the Tebu as labourers and extending its trading route into the Wadai, now part of Chad. It is said that Kufra under their rule was the most noted centre of brigandage in the Sahara.

Today, al-Zawiya tribe commands the trade, legal and illegal, that passes through the Kufra oasis archipelago and along the only tarmac road from thence to Jalo in the north.

It was into this complex and hierarchical tribal system that Khalifa Haftar was born. His father was a prominent member of the al-Farjan tribe, a client tribe of a special nature due to its being classed as one of the Marabtin bil baraka, 'the tribes of the blessing'. They, like others such as the Aulad al-Sheik and the Masamir, live among the Sa'adi tribes as equals because of their supposed descent from saints. This means that Haftar's tribe is held in high regard as having religious rather than secular esteem. It allows them to live as near equals among several tribes without paying for the land and water. The Farjanis are respected by all the tribes they live among and are thus not perceived as partisan, an advantage which Haftar would later find invaluable in negotiations. The Sa'adis, however, do not regard them as quite 'like themselves' as they are not of Bedouin descent, their ancestor having supposedly migrated into Libya from the Maghreb. This is indeed possible, as pilgrims to and from Mecca made their way by land through Libya and some may well have settled there.

It will not have escaped the notice of the more diligent diplomats or intelligence analysts that the Farjanis live not only among the al-Ghaddfa, the Awlad Suleiman, the al-Magharba and the al-Awaquir tribes in the area stretching from Sirte in the west to Benghazi in the east, but are also a close neighbour of the al-Zawiya tribe to their south. This meant that Haftar's fellow tribesmen could be found from Sirte all the way to Benghazi. Indeed, Haftar's brother is today the leader of the Benghazi Farjanis. Haftar was born into a family with a 'special relationship' with the tribes not only in the north, but also as far south as Sebha through the Awlad Suleiman. They also had a good neighbourly relationship with the al-Zawiya tribe, which extended potential alliances as far as Kufra in the south-east. Political relationships as far-reaching as this were seldom seen in Libya.

Haftar's mother, on the other hand, was said to have Egyptian connections as well as her relationship with the Sway. Marriage in Libya did, and may still, create obligations and debts arising from what is known as the bride price. Transactions today which take place in arranged marriages are complicated but usually of a local nature, so Haftar's relationships gave him a wider sphere of international influence than was normal. Later in life his link to Egypt, and particularly Egypt's feeling towards the British, would prove crucial.

The relationship between Libya, Egypt and the British in 1942 was complex. Even as early as 1941, when the British planned for war in Cyrenaica, they were forced to consider how to ensure the Libyan people were on their side. Fighting where there is a hostile civilian population has obvious downsides, and good intelligence from behind enemy lines was essential.

While the British were fighting in Libya, tucked away quietly in Alexandria was the exiled hereditary leader of the Senussi sect, Sayyid Idris al-Senussi. The descendant of the impressively named

Al-Sayyid Muhammad bin 'Ali al-Senussi al-Khattabi al-Idrisi al-Hasani, now known as the Grand Senussi, Idris al-Senussi was one of a long line of distinguished Algerians claiming descent from the Prophet Mohammad himself. For a short while Idris al-Senussi had been appointed Emir of Cyrenaica by the Italian colonists and was destined to become King of Libya when it became fully independent. But in 1931 the Italians had built up sufficient strength to project their power across the desert and they attacked his stronghold in the Kufra oasis and brutally killed the Senussi supporters there. Idris al-Senussi went into exile in Egypt, but his position as the first and last king of Libya was, for some, intact.

With Idris al-Senussi in Egypt were several Cyrenaica sheiks and 14,000 Libyans also in exile from Italian colonial rule. In October 1939, when it seemed certain that Italy would invade Egypt, these exiled sheiks had met in Alexandria and formally recognised Idris as their emir. They told the British ambassador in Egypt that Idris could speak for them in all negotiations. When Italy declared war, the sheiks met again in Cairo and decided to raise a Libyan Arab Force to fight alongside the British Army in the Western Desert.

Idris al-Senussi and the Libyan Sheiks sided with the British. They expected the British to reciprocate: for them to declare Idris the future ruler of an independent Cyrenaica. Was this a promise the British could make? The Egyptians were not enthusiastically committed to the British cause and were already laying claim to a post-war Cyrenaica. There were also, of course, German spies and sympathisers in Cairo and when British fortunes were looking bleak anti-British sentiment was expressed openly in high society circles and among the officers of the Egyptian Army. The Muslim Brotherhood, an Islamic political and grassroots social organisation started in Egypt in 1928, was beginning to popularise and mobilise resentment about British arrogance.

On 8 January 1942 the British government declared that 'His Majesty's Government is determined that at the end of the war the Senussis of Cyrenaica will in no circumstances again fall under Italian domination'. It was as far as they were prepared to go. The declaration fell short of backing a future independent Cyrenaica, but it was a trump card of sorts. Idris was to parlay it into a successful claim to the Kingdom of Libya over the next decade.

The timing of Haftar's birth, into an influential tribe with powerful affiliations to its neighbours, couldn't have been more significant. As the British gained control of post-Italian Libya, still the hangover of centuries of colonial rule remained. But there were signs that the British Empire was becoming senescent and its control of what is now called the Middle East was already weakening. While Britain was eventually successful in winning the war in the desert, its position as a great power was fatally eroded. In Egypt, the forces which were unleashed throughout much of the Arab world by the catastrophe of the Second World War were gathering in the Egyptian Army around Gamal Abdul Nasser and Anwar Sadat, both of whom were to become presidents of Egypt, and the tortuous negotiations which would bring Idris al-Senussi to power in Libya were underway. The Muslim Brotherhood, founded in 1928, was slowly but surely gaining influence and political presence. With its Egyptian connections, Haftar's family would have been aware of these events, which would eventually lead to Libya's independence. But who would lead the free Libya, and how?

Just seventeen months previous to Haftar's birth another baby had been born, this time in a Bedouin tent pitched near Quasr Abu Hadi, where the Sahara meets the Mediterranean. The boy was named Muammar, and he inherited the tribal name of Ghaddafi.

Throughout their childhood, adolescence and early manhood, both boys would watch the British rule their country. They would see how the machinations and manoeuvring begun well before they were born would come together to promote the leader of the Senussi sect to the kingship of Libya. But there were other forces already in play, forces that would destroy the monarchy, bring Ghaddafi to power and divide Libya for decades.

2

OFFICERS, GENTLEMEN AND PLOTTERS

As the second half of the twentieth century unfolded, the influence of the British and US military bases on the Libyan people waned and the effect of the great oil reserves below the desert hinterland grew. To have lived through part of that period and to look back upon it in the light of Libya's present agony leads to a striking but simple conclusion: Libya's future was in foreign hands. Is it still?

The spectacular and precious ruins of Roman and Greek cities which became just part of the scenery as one travelled around send a message which is hard to silence. Add this to the debris and detritus of the battles of the Second World War, which lingered in East Libya in particular, and the message becomes more insistent, especially so if one caught a fleeting glimpse of Bedouin tents or police patrolling the desert fringes on camels. Where were the Libyan people when all this was played out in their homelands?

At this time, in Tobruk, the frail King of Libya lived in a modest palace. He was the descendant of an Algerian religious leader who had founded a theocracy in the Libyan desert and it had been politicised in the course of a war between great foreign powers fought out in the homelands of Libyan Bedouin tribes. He too was foreign – in terms of arbitrary national boundaries drawn by colonial powers, that is. Can the Libya he helped to forge survive intact?

As I write, a proxy war rages in Libya between the Turks on one side and the Russians on the other. Libyan people live and try to work within sight or earshot of war whilst the future of their country is discussed between foreign powers who remain unable to reach an agreement. The problems they wrestle with are familiar to those their predecessors struggled with in the middle decades of the twentieth century. Will the displaced and the traumatised victims of war have a tranquil home in which to live and raise their progeny?

What follows is a brief story of events that led to the formation of an independent state called Libya and a little of the early life of a soldier called Khalifa Haftar who was born in Ajdabiya and of his sometime hero and later enemy, Muammar Ghaddafi, who was born in a tent near Sirte.

A Libyan Army Is Raised in Wartime Egypt Which Helps the Sufi Emir Idris al-Senussi Become King of Libya

Why is the history of the Libyan Army relevant today? I suggest that there are two reasons to devote time to a brief review of its origin. The obvious one is that it trained Khalifa Haftar and he served it with distinction, as we will see. In the last few years, he has raised an army which he boasts is its direct descendent. It brought him into contact with Muammar Ghaddafi who used it to propel himself to power, gave him experience of command and, especially, the taste of defeat and humiliation. Now, as Field Marshal Khalifa Haftar, he leads an army which has a number of interesting elements. There are tribal militias from the city of Zintan in the Western Mountains and Tebu militias from the south. Controversially, there are said to be a number of mercenary militias from Chad and Darfur province in the Sudan. Russian Wagner mercenaries are under his command and recently he has been accused of importing Syrian militias. At the heart of his force there are regular Libyan Army units and regular Libyan Army officers on whom he relies.

The Libyan Army had its origin in Cairo during the Second World War. Its first recruits were Libyan exiles in Egypt who had escaped from the Italian colonial regime in Libya. It was first called the Senussi Arab Force but soon became the Libyan Arab Force. Its first name reflects the fact that it was formed at the request of the exiled Emir Idris al-Senussi and it became the principal lever which he used to become King of Libya when it became an independent nation in 1951.

There is a more important reason. The formation of the Libyan Army is acknowledged to have taken place in Egypt. The story of its origin reflects the stresses and turbulence which bedevil Libya today so closely. It is thus profitable to follow its early history to help us discern the origins of Libya's present murderous dilemma. It is also a pointer to what I and others have noted. That is the extent to which what we might call outside forces influenced the formation of Libya the nation and why it is, at the time of writing, the target of a proxy war while foreign states battle over its resources. Is the idea of Libya as a nation still not sufficiently lodged in the imagination of the Libyan people to heal the fissures which are so evident today, or is a strongman the only solution in the short run at least?

At some time during the First World War the Emir Idris al-Senussi impressed the British in some sensitive negotiation in the matter of the frontier between Libya and Egypt in which the Senussi holy city of Jaghbub was involved. The story of these negotiations reads like a novel by the masters of British Imperialist fiction such as John Buchan or R. A. Henty. The upshot was that Emir Idris was trusted by the British based in Cairo in the early stages of the Second World War and, crucially, decided that his future political ambitions in Libya would be best served by an alliance with Britain.

As we have seen, Emir Idris and other members of the Senussi family were forced into exile in 1930 when the Italian colonists successfully attacked Kufra, their oasis stronghold deep in the Libyan desert. They established themselves in Alexandria where they became the trusted leaders of the Libyan refugee community in Egypt. There were a number of Libyan tribal sheiks who were also in exile in Egypt, though it must be said that most of them were from East Libya, then known as Cyrenaica. The reason for this is that the Cyrenaican sheiks had led a guerrilla war against the Italian colonists who had occupied much of their fertile tribal homelands and had incarcerated Bedouin families in concentration camps. The Tripolitanian sheiks had not exiled themselves because the relationship between them and the Italian colonist was less antagonistic and there was less cohesion among their tribes. The Tripolitanian tribes were inclined to throw in their hand with the Italians.

It is the relative cohesion between the Cyrenaican tribes and the notable lack of it between the Tripolitanian tribes which is evident today and is one of the main reasons why the efforts to broker a peaceful solution to Libya's brutal civil war are so far unrewarding. It must also be said that the distance between Tripoli and Alexandria is considerable and the desolate country around the south of the Gulf of Sirte discourages east–west road travel – even today. It is also important to emphasise that East Libya has always orientated towards Egypt and the Arab east whilst West Libya leans towards the Maghreb.

In 1940 the British position in the Middle East was weak. The Axis powers were in the ascendancy in Europe and German propaganda was making inroads into Egyptian high society. The fledgling Muslim Brotherhood was making anti-British propaganda among ordinary Egyptians. The Egyptian King Farouk's government refused the overtures of the powerful British ambassador, Sir Miles Lampson, to declare war on Germany and Italy despite an Italian army on Egyptian soil and attacking Egyptian Army bases. The fall of France on 22 June 1940 changed the balance of naval power in the Mediterranean and military power in the Maghreb.

Emir Idris exploited the British weakness. On 1 July 1940 he held a secret meeting with the General Officer Commanding the British forces in Egypt and, significantly, Lieutenant Colonel Bromilow, during which he offered his support for the immediate formation of a Libyan exile force to fight the Italians in Libya providing they would undertake its organisation and control.

On 5 July 1940 the British War Office gave permission for the formation of up to ten battalions of 'Senussi' tribesmen from among the Libyan refugees in Egypt. There were to be five hundred men per battalion with British and Libyan officers. The Egyptian government gave its grudging approval on 9 July with the caveat that it would not be involved. Grudging because the Egyptians were protecting their neutrality should Italy defeat the British.

Two battalions were rapidly raised under the command of Lieutenant Colonel Bromilow and called the Senussi Arab Force. This title was soon changed to widen its recruiting base to the Libyan Arab Force. I do not think I am alone in asserting that this was the origin of the Libyan Army. I heard the point made by senior Libyan Army officers during the handover of Tripoli's Bab al-Aziziya barracks from the Royal Irish Fusiliers to the Libyan Army sometime in 1960 – an event of some considerable significance in the history of the Libyan Army.

Emir Idris clearly needed a mandate. He had already called a meeting of exiled Libyan sheiks on 8 August in Cairo's Garden City and hijacked the outcome by opening proceedings on the 7th knowing that two prominent Tripolitanian sheiks who would oppose him had yet to arrive. Thus, he obtained a signed agreement of twenty-one of the twenty-five Libyan sheiks to the formation of a Libyan Arab Force to fight alongside and to be financed by the British and owing its loyalty to him.

In return for his support Emir Idris asked the British to announce that Libya would become a British protectorate immediately after the defeat of the Italians and to declare the future independence of Libya as an autonomous emirate, naturally with him as emir, and in so doing neutralised Egypt's ambitions in the post-war carve-up of her western neighbour.

One intriguing story emerges from sources close to Emir Idris at the time. He revealed the Tripolitanian sheiks began to change their view as the British 8th Army swept Erwin Rommel's defeated forces towards Tripoli early in 1943. They made backchannel approaches to him through Abdul Sattar Bey al-Basil, an Egyptian senator with strong Cyrenaican family connections with Libya. They were trying to establish a reconciliation with Emir Idris and, not the least consideration I am sure, with a future British Military Government in Tripolitania. They may have realised that the Italians would make a case for retaining Tripolitania once Mussolini's fascist government had been replaced by one more acceptable to the British. This eventuality was not as unlikely as it first appeared. The British had been attempting to court anti-fascist support in Italy, and in the Italian army in Libya, by means of intensive propaganda. The sheiks clearly saw that as a threat to their hopes of throwing off the Italian yoke and achieving independence. They may have decided that the prospect of Idris al-Senussi, favoured as he was by the British, as Emir of Libya entire was preferable to the Italians. This seemingly obscure intrigue helps us understand the difficulties experienced by those who negotiated Libya's independence in 1951, and more importantly the tangled loyalties and animosities which bedevil Libya today. It also hints at the growing importance of Emir Idris and his Libyan Arab Force in the future of Libya.

The newly raised Libyan Arab Force was deployed in Libya for the first time in December 1940. A first British Military Administration of Cyrenaica was set up between December 1940 and February 1941. It found that though many Italian colonists had left, a number had remained, especially and fortunately those who had small agricultural holdings in the fertile areas of the Green Mountains. These smallholdings had been planted in the homelands of some of the powerful tribes whose members had been put into concentration camps. The British Military Administration was in an unenviable position. The Libyan Bedouin who had been removed by force from their homeland to make way for the farmers were semi-nomadic pastoralists. They were unable to take over the farms. There was an acute food shortage and it was necessary to keep the Italian settlers in their farms and producing food. They needed protection. The Libyan Arab Force was drafted in to do the job.

The contribution that the Libyan Arab Force made was summed up by a masterful wordsmith in the British Foreign Office for Anthony Eden, the Foreign Secretary who made this announcement in Parliament. It is one of the most important statements in Libya's modern history. Here it is from *Hansard* dated 8 January 1942:

Mr Emrys Evans asked the Secretary of State for Foreign Affairs whether he will make a statement in respect of the Senussis having regard to their co-operation with His Majesty's forces in the Western Desert?

Mr. Eden: Yes, Sir. The Sayid Idris el Senussi made contact with the British authorities in Egypt within a month of the collapse of France, at a time when the military situation in Africa was most unfavourable to us. A Senussi Force was subsequently raised from those of his followers who had escaped from Italian oppression at various times during the past twenty years. This force performed considerable ancillary duties during the successful fighting in the Western Desert in the winter of 1940–41 and is again playing a useful part in the campaign now in progress. I take this opportunity to express the warm appreciation of His Majesty's Government for the contribution which Sayid Idris el Senussi and his followers have made and are making to the British war effort. We welcome their association with His Majesty's Forces in the task of defeating the common enemies. His Majesty's Government are determined that at the end of the war the Senussis in Cyrenaica will in no circumstances again fall under Italian domination.

The striking reference to the Senussis rather than the people of Cyrenaica is noted. It was taken as a guarded reference to the future role of the Senussi sect in Libya. From here on the Senussis had a promise they would use with tenacity and determination. The 3rd British Military Administration of Cyrenaica was to act on the promise. The upshot was that Idris al-Senussi became King of Libya in 1951. Both Muammar Ghaddafi and Khalifa Haftar joined that Libyan Army in order to use it to bring down the monarchy.

Calm Green Mountains – Unforgiving Desert

I am 'miked up' and sitting next to George Alagiah, the anchorman for the BBC national and international news bulletin. Colonel Ghadaffi has been killed and I am to talk for four minutes about his second son, Saif al-Islam al-Ghaddafi, then imprisoned in Zintan up in Libya's Western Mountains, the Jebel Nefusa. There is a pause in the studio while an intrepid reporter does his stuff and so Mr Alagiah quizzes me about the strangeness of Saif's father. I explain my hypothesis, which is that his early life and adolescence was spent in profound isolation. Mr Alagiah did not seem to agree. He received a word from his producer and suddenly we were broadcasting to millions. Why do our youthful experiences matter so much? Because it is then that the part of our brain which supervises our mores is still forming. Because Muammar Ghaddafi dominated Libya for forty-two years and Khalifa Haftar is a potential strongman who bids for power as I write. Here is a brief comparison of their early lives; I leave you to judge.

Ajdabiya town was busy with a war when Haftar was born. It was not his war or that of his tribe but its alien drumbeat was his constant companion. He first attended a primary school in Ajdabiya. In 1961 he packed his kit and travelled to Derna where he attended school until 1964 when he qualified to compete for a place at the Royal Libyan Military Academy in Benghazi.

Derna is a port some 450 kilometres north-east of Ajdabiya by road today. To reach it he will have travelled through the Green Mountains, still strewn with the ruins of ancient Cyrene, until they dip towards the plain in which the city lies. The last part of the journey was down the steep and narrow 'Z' bends with a yawning abyss on one side and scrub on the other.

Derna was relatively unharmed in the Second World War. That is why it was a clean and pleasant city in 1961. It was, and still is, spared the extremes of temperature Haftar would have been used to at home. It was well supplied by sweet and abundant water which flows from the Green Mountains through the drainage channels into the sea and which irrigated, in Haftar's school days, an abundance of fruit trees and supplied the majority of households unstintingly. I note that Haftar is an accomplished linguist and may well have been well taught by good linguists at school. I recall working with a Libyan from Derna who, when he chaired our regular meetings, used English, Italian, French and Arabic fluently to include the polyglot group with whom we worked.

Derna became famous for producing a surprising number of militant Islamists during Ghaddafi's regime and was occupied recently by a brutal Islamist militia which caused Haftar's most experienced soldiers much time and trouble to remove. Haftar's battle for Derna will be the subject of a later chapter but it is strange how the city could produce the most civilised and capable men and attract the most brutal of militants.

Khalifa Haftar's early life in Ajdabiya and Derna contrasts sharply with that of Muammar Ghaddafi, who was to have a profound effect on his life, and on Libya. In many ways Haftar has lived his life framed by and in opposition to Ghaddafi. Comparing their early lives may shed some light on the roots of Libya's descent into civil strife.

The old Italian colonial road had been built around the shores of the Gulf of Sirte which thrusts its way into the desert. If you look at the map, you can see that there are really two Gulfs of Sirte, the lesser and the greater. The map makes them look like two successive mouthfuls taken out of the north coast of Libya. The road is long and the desert desolate and, if you allow yourself to think too much, it is very intimidating. At the southern reach of the Gulf is the town of Sirte.

When I was in the region in 1961, Sirte's isolation was truly stunning. Ghaddafi was born here, in one of the tents of the al-Ghaddadfa tribe which made its meagre living in its harsh desert hinterland. Recollections of his birthplace, the Bedouin ways of his parents and the importance of the tribe in his culture had been built up in his memory and self-edited over the years to establish his personal narrative, the personal story he carried in his head.

Here is the narrative, as it emerged in 2002, which Ghaddafi had prepared for public consumption. On 2 November of that year, he was interviewed in his tent in Azzizia Barracks by Professor Edmond Jouve. The transcript of the interview appears in *My Vision* by Muammar Ghaddafi and Edmond Jouve. Ghaddafi is reported to have said, 'I was born in a tent in the desert in September 1942. There was no doctor or midwife present. I went to school fairly late. I didn't give it any thought. I was guarding the herds, sowing the seed, cultivating the land.' This is a summary of the life of an adolescent boy in a Bedouin tent, though some of the tasks described would have been reserved for older boys. In the same interview Ghaddafi implies that he and his family were not aware of the concept of a state or a government.

Ghaddafi was to make much of his tribal roots and affiliations. His own tribe, the Ghaddadfa, were said to be of Arab–Berber blood, and he was conscious of this and the way it was perceived, especially by the Sa'adi tribes so dominant when he was young. Its homeland reaches from the shores of the Gulf of Sirte through the dry, unforgiving and desiccated desert towards Sebha and it coincides with that of the powerful Awlad Suleman tribe which has strong connections in the Sahel. There is also a close connection with the warlike, lordly and independent Warfella tribe centred on the mountain city called Bani Walid. The homeland of the Ghaddadfa tribe spans the political frontier between East and West Libya, an arbitrary line of demarcation drawn by Libya's sometime colonial masters. Ghaddafi's pan-Arabism and his pan-Africanism had their roots in the Ghaddadfa's homeland.

In his *Green Book*, written as a manifesto, Ghaddafi devoted two sections to the tribe. He argued that '(the tribe) is a social school where its members are brought up from childhood to absorb high ideals which will be transformed into a behaviour pattern for life ... the tribe provides for its members ... collective payment of ransom, collective fines, collective revenge and collective defence.'[1]

---

1. Muammar Ghaddafi and Edmond Jouve, *My Vision* (London: John Blake, 2005), p. 154

In his interview with Professor Jouve, he recalled the Second World War and he described exploding mines, flying bullets and aerial bombardments. These would have been folk memories, for he would have been too young to have been an eyewitness, unless he had falsified his birth date. That he did not understand the reason for it all is not surprising. It was a war fought in Libya between foreigners for reasons that the tribesmen would not have welcomed. 'Those were my earliest childhood memories,' Ghaddafi told Professor Jouve. That they were not accurate is of little consequence. They formed part of his core person and affected his adult behaviour.[2]

When he lived in his parents' tent Ghaddafi was given some religious education by a tribal teacher. If that is so this will have taken the form of rote learning. Probably at the age of ten Ghaddafi left the family tent and enrolled in the primary school in Sirte. He made good progress but was ridiculed because he was a Bedouin. He later moved to Sebha in the Fezzan where his father took a post as a caretaker guarding a prominent citizen's property. Ghaddafi entered a secondary school in the town and embarked on a revolutionary career. He came into contact with Egyptian teachers and under the influence of Nasser's Voice of the Arabs on the radio.

He was expelled from the school in Sebha and there are conflicting stories as to why. They all focus on his political activity, which consisted of giving speeches, distributing leaflets and, some say, being gratuitously rude to an English school inspector. Whatever the reason, he moved to a secondary school in Misrata, where he met a number of his fellow conspirators with whom he was to overthrow the king. He is said to have formed the nucleus of his revolutionary band of officers here. They all decided to obtain commissions in the army, which they

---

2. Ibid, pp. 81, 82

proposed to take over and use as the instrument of their coup and as their power base afterwards.

The modern world arrived in one blow for the Libyan Bedouins. It came from outside and was not spread over three or four centuries. The cultural gulf which the young Ghaddafi and his fellow revolutionaries crossed between the Bedouin tents and the two major Libyan cities, Tripoli and Benghazi, was wide indeed. We might step back over that gulf to understand Ghaddafi a little better.

When he came to power Ghaddafi was sometimes ridiculed because he pitched his Bedouin tent near his home in Azzizia Barracks and frequently threatened to cart it around with him on international trips. It caused consternation wherever he proposed to take it. It was hard to find a place safe enough for it in Cairo or New York without risking some sort of security or sanitary incident. In reality his tent was largely symbolic. He was making his Bedouin origins clear to the world.

Haftar Enters the Royal Libyan Military College and Attracts the Attention of Muammar Ghaddafi

Before taking the story further it is pertinent to ask, for the first time, what drives Haftar and what sustains him in adversity? We can discern some of his traits and understand part of his motivation by putting his early training into a Libyan context. There is a plethora of books about leadership and a number of media stars offer plausible advice on how to be one. The British military, drawing on years of experience and the example of notable leaders, teaches the basic skills of the art to its officer cadets in long-established institutions such as the Royal Military Academy at Sandhurst, the Royal Naval College, Dartmouth, and latterly, the Royal Air Force College, Cranwell. In the USA, training officers at West Point is a long and hallowed tradition.

In the 1960s an officer cadet in the British Royal Military Academy, providing he survived the course, could look forward to a career in one of the leading armies in the world led by men with wide experience and in which promotion was gained by merit, though in some regiments good connections were helpful. He could expect to be posted overseas to serve in Germany, Cyprus, or in the more exotic reaches of what remained of the British Empire and Commonwealth. The people who trained him were chosen with care and he had heroes enough from the past glories of British history. When he completed his training he received the queen's commission and thus owed his loyalty to his monarch who, by virtue of his commission, he represented, and received a salute as such from the soldiers he commanded. Thus, he was required to relegate his political life to the recesses of his mind and obey the instructions of Her Majesty's Government whatever its political stripe.

Haftar entered the Royal Libyan Military Academy in September 1964. What motivated him to do so? He has not shared his motivations widely. He enrolled, he is quoted as saying, as the best way to 'change the monarchical regime' and to 'confront our true and sole enemy, the Zionists'. He also claimed to be a 'fervent believer' in the philosophy of the Egyptian president Gamal Abdul Nasser. It was these views that caught the attention of Muammar Ghaddafi, who was recruiting cadets into his plot to overthrow the monarchy.

Khalifa Haftar was a cadet at the Royal Libyan Military Academy in Benghazi at a time when British training methods were still in use. Though he later trained in Russia it is the British influence on his early training which I am sure he acknowledges in the rank of Field Marshal that he has awarded himself. I detect in his bearing and his attitude when inspecting his troops that of a British trained officer of the old days when they were probably the best military trainers in the world.

I am sure he was successful but his natural reserve would have disguised, for a while, what the British refer to as his officer qualities. Under pressure his fatalism, tenacity and indifference to danger would have become clear. After long immersion in Libyan culture I assert that these are Libyan traits and stem from his faith. The directing staff may have noted that he was capable of anger if thwarted but no one at the time would have seen him as the man who could walk out of a conference with Putin and Erdogan or that he would be bidding to become the strongman saviour of Libya.

Haftar's role in the Ghaddafi-led putsch on 1 September 1969 has been obfuscated by hurried journalists. There are some reports which make claims on his behalf, not all of which are to his advantage. He has been personally circumspect in his claims to fame but, as with most of us, it is possible to find contradictions in his statements of intent. Some reports suggest that he was a member of Ghaddafi's close circle of plotters at the RLMA. That is not so, as we have seen. He attracted their attention, and admits to admiring Ghaddafi, supporting the plot against King Idris and feeling hatred for Zionists. He was not a member of the core group of twelve which was to form the Revolutionary Command Council which planned the coup. They had been with Ghaddafi for some time. He was deemed trustworthy enough, and that is important for plotters. As a result, he was admitted to the Free Officers, who were tasked with the onerous but lesser role of implementing the plans drawn up by the Revolutionary Command Council.

I offer these anecdotes to illustrate the danger and tension the twelve plotters were under and the care they took when choosing the Free Officers. I must declare an interest. Sometime in the last century the officers of the British Military Mission to Libya hired a villa a short distance from our home in Benghazi in which to house their officer's mess and where they could unwind among themselves and occasionally their lady wives, though in keeping with the traditions of the British military at that time the wives were infrequent guests.

In 1961 the officers were kind enough to invite me to be an honorary member and I would thereafter enjoy a cold beer or two and the exchange of anecdotes about the pressures of working in Libya. Since I, and the officers of the mission, signed the Official Secrets Act I hasten to add that what follows can be found and corroborated in the many excellent histories of Libya still for sale in your local bookshop. I have refreshed my memories about that interesting time from a number of such books.

The mission was led by Colonel Ted Lough, a wise and battle-hardened officer late of the Parachute Regiment. He was an officer of notable judgement and integrity. Among his duties he advised the Libyan Army Colonel Commandant in command of the Royal Libyan Military College in Benghazi. Haftar entered the college in September 1964, a year after Muammar Ghaddafi.

Ted was unimpressed by Officer Cadet Muammar Ghaddafi, who was clearly less than interested in his studies. He had other things on his mind. Ghaddafi and a number of his fellow cadets at the Royal Libyan Military College were plotting to emulate their hero Gamal Abdul Nasser and form the clandestine Free Officer's Movement which was to join him in his putsch and take over the government of Libya when King Idris abdicated in 1969. Among these young men was Officer Cadet Khalifa Haftar, though I heard nothing about him that I can recall.

Someone shot the Libyan Colonel Commandant. Ted Lough visited him on his deathbed. He whispered something to Ted which was barely audible. Ted Lough was near certain he said 'Muammar'. The murderer was never identified. Officer Cadet Muammar Ghaddafi was re-coursed for a year, having failed to impress his instructors.

There was a British Army NCO in the British Military Mission who sported a notable moustache and was said to chew glass when among convivial friends in the Sergeants' Mess. He was a qualified range instructor and thus trained officer cadets at the RLMA to shoot. He was less than amused when a cadet was fatally shot during a range practice which he was supervising. He was convinced that the shooting was deliberate, but the perpetrators claimed it was accidental. Though he was a colourful character many of us shared his professional view and speculated about the motive. In hindsight the victim may have tried to betray the plotters. The plotters only had to kill once to raise the cost of betrayal. You may want to treat this anecdote with caution but I understand that the incident was reported to the British Embassy.

Abdul Gamal Nasser Readjusts the Arab World; Hassan al-Banna Squares the Circle

When the Suez crisis occurred in late 1956 I was a young RAF officer. For the first time – and the last – I heard a senior RAF officer openly criticise Her Majesty's Government. For such a thing to happen at all there must have been something wrong. There was if you were British, for it signalled the end of the Empire as you knew it. For Muammar Ghaddafi and Khalifa Haftar, it was the beginning of something.

When Khalifa Haftar was young, Abdul Gamal Nasser held sway in Egypt and his propaganda was spread by radio across the Libyan Desert and by Egyptian teachers in Libyan schools. It should surprise no one that Nasser was Ghaddafi's and Haftar's hero. Ahmad Said, the head of Nasser's radio station, Voice of the Arabs, was the voice that the young men of the tribes listened to with notable results. Khalifa Haftar could hardly have escaped his unscrupulous but brilliant propaganda. It was virulently anti-colonial and notably anti-British.

There are a number of ways in which Nasser's influence was to play out in Haftar's life and on the life of his onetime friend and leader Muammar Ghaddafi. What were they? Haftar and Ghaddafi, like their hero Nasser, were to join the army and use it to foment a putsch which toppled a king.

Nasser, the son of a postmaster, was accepted as an officer cadet into the Egyptian Military Academy in 1937, together with most of those who were to form a group called the Free Officers who were to be his power base in the future. The Military Academy had been for the sons of Beys and Pashas, but it opened its doors to cadets with secondary school leaving certificates and leadership potential. Most of Nasser's Free Officers had also benefitted from this change in selection policy. As a cadet, Nasser was a voracious reader of history, politics and biography. Ghaddafi has often stated that he too read widely. The immediate aims of the revolutionary movement which Nasser was to lead were thus developed after considerable research by a man of great intelligence and immense mental energy. These aims were neither Marxist nor Islamist but fervently nationalistic. They were secular.

Nasser was determined to overthrow the Egyptian monarchy, then personified by the sybaritic King Farouk. He was also determined to remove the British military occupation of his country and to redistribute to the *fellaheen* (peasants) the fertile land which was mostly in the hands of a few landowners. For his part, Ghaddafi was to remove King Idris, get rid of the British and US military bases from Libya and break the hold of the big oil companies on the only real source of wealth in his otherwise impoverished homeland.

Nasser's chance came when King Farouk's Wafdist Party government was in some political trouble. It had decided that an anti-British stance would ensure support, so it abrogated the 1936 Anglo-Egyptian Treaty, arranged for the 30,000 civilian workers to leave the British Army in the lurch in the Canal Zone and encouraged sabotage and terrorist attacks on British military establishments. This had the effect of neutralising the strategic value of the Canal Zone because the British military effort was taken up in compensating for the loss of Egyptian labour and in self-defence.

Predictably the British failed to appreciate the situation. Riots broke out in Cairo and many British-owned properties and iconic buildings were attacked and torched, including the famous Shepherd's Hotel. This incident sounded the death knell for King Farouk and his government, and the Free Officers, nominally headed by the distinguished General Muhammad Naguib, decided to seize power in 1952. The British, who were not enamoured of Farouk and his government, were probably lulled into a sense of security by Naguib and did nothing to intervene. This was to be another strange parallel with the British unexpected failure to intervene in Ghaddafi's coup in Libya.

The Egyptian Free Officers formed a Revolutionary Command Council with Naguib as its chairman and set about consolidating their power. By the end of 1954, Nasser had removed Naguib and was in undisputed control of Egypt. That year he published a book called *The Philosophy of Revolution*. Once again, we can draw parallels with Ghaddafi and his Revolutionary Command Council in Libya and his publication of the *Green Book*.

The result was the straw that broke the British Imperial camel's back. In a state of a dangerously obsessive dislike of Nasser, which appears to some to have destroyed his judgement, the British Prime Minster, Anthony Eden, launched an Angelo-French invasion of Egypt. On 5 November 1957, the British, with Israeli and French support, landed in Suez, and one of the most ignominious campaigns fought by the British for a number of years commenced. Eden was ill with prostate trouble. The USA was not amused and put irresistible pressure on the British to withdraw, as did some Commonwealth governments.

Russia joined in with condemnation and the British forces were withdrawn without honour. Britain and France no longer commanded the vital Suez Canal and Britain's bluff had been called by the son of an Egyptian post office clerk.

For Libya, heavily dependent on the presence of British troops, the situation was fraught, but in much of the Arab world the humiliation of the British was received with acclamation. But the Libyan children of the Bedouin tents and the tin huts in the towns listened on their transistor radios to Umm Kalthoum, the Egyptian singer, the most famous of her time, and dubbed the opium of the Arabs. Her songs, some of which could last for two hours, drew audiences from all over the Arab-speaking world to the Voice of the Arabs and Nasser's propaganda. She died in her late seventies in February 1975. I suggest that the effect on Ghaddafi and Haftar of Umm Kalthoum and Ahmad Said were profound. Nasser was of the people. He directed his propaganda at the *fellaheen*, the domestic servant, the bus driver and the docker and he repeated this phrase which hits straight home in Arabic but loses much in translation: 'Raise your head fellow brother – the end of colonialism has come.' These words were broadcast across the desert to where Muammar Ghaddafi was at school in Sebha and across Libya's Green Mountains to Derna where Khalifa Haftar was a young scholar.

While emulating Nasser in preparing their military coup, Ghaddafi and his fellow cadets at the Royal Libyan Military Academy in Benghazi must have spent a great deal of their free time sounding out friends and foes and making plans. His core group was called the Free Officers Movement, as had been Nasser's conspirators in the Egyptian army. The loyalty of many of his early conspirators was assured because they had joined the army for the express purpose of mounting a coup.

In 1954 Nasser was shot eight times whilst delivering a speech. He survived. The would-be assassin was deemed to have been a member of the Muslim Brotherhood. As a result, six members of the Brotherhood were executed and many imprisoned. It was Hassan al-Banna who founded the Muslim Brotherhood, in Egypt in 1928. He was, by all accounts an eloquent and magnetic character, charismatic perhaps. He could 'walk with kings nor lose the common touch'. Some say he was a social chameleon but he was a good organiser. He knew well that his movement would not succeed in Egypt unless he made an accommodation with powerful people. He was notably energetic and travelled widely, recruiting among the ordinary people. He encouraged his members to undertake community and social service and recruited a near-paramilitary youth movement which was notably disciplined and increasingly turned to violence against the British. The sybaritic high society and the superiority of the British irked ordinary Egyptians and made them ready recruits who were uneasy about the moral decline of Egyptian society. He encouraged the establishment of numerous branches whose members undertook the indoctrination of new members and he began calling on the monarch and the establishment to institute Shari'ah law. His influence spiralled across the Middle East. He was killed in February 1949, probably by Egyptian security police. It did not make headway against the Senussis in neighbouring East Libya. Ghaddafi banned it (of which more later). The Muslim Brotherhood came to power in Egypt in 2012 but its tenure was short. It has been successful in Libya since the 2011 uprising and remains so in Turkey and Qatar.

Cambridge Blues, Indirect Rule, Gallic Ambitions; Something about the British and French Military Administrations in Libya

I met Sir Duncan Cumming twice in Libya and once in Papua. In those brief encounters he sparked my interest in Libyan tribes. There has been little close and detailed survey of the tribes as they

*are today so most of us rely on the work of the Italian Colonel di
Agostini and that of the notable Professor E. E. Evans-Pritchard.
The latter was an important member of Duncan Cumming's
staff in the British Military Administration of Cyrenaica. For me
it was the protection of Mohamed al-Abbar of the al-Awaquir
tribe that saw me through some testing times but whose generous
hospitality led to some intestinal discord.*

In May 1942, while Erwin Rommel was leading his Panzer Corps
Africa into Egypt, Brigadier Duncan Cumming was appointed
Deputy Chief Political Officer for Cyrenaica and based in Cairo.
He worked alongside the Arabic-speaking Norman Anderson,
who was the Political Officer for Senussi Affairs. Idris al-Senussi
could not speak English (a problem which was not helpful then
and later when he was ruling oil-rich Libya). Cumming and
Anderson were faced with an interesting challenge.

They were to form the third British Military Administration
of the Italian province of Cyrenaica, assuming it was recaptured.
Military governments of territories captured in warfare were
given legitimacy by the Hague Convention of 1906, which
allowed them to govern on a care-and-maintenance basis. But
many of the Italians had already left and the Libyans who
inhabited the province were not enemies. To the British, the
Italian colonists were the enemy and the Libyans were the friends
who had rendered service to the British military and formed
the Libyan Arab Force. The second problem was the post-war
future of Cyrenaica. It was not a simple matter and was not fully
resolved until 1951. The third was how to govern a huge country
which was likely to be devastated by war. With no skilled and
experienced Libyan administrators, no political system and no
farmers, the last was to test the BMA severely – as we will see.

In addition to these pressing and unusual dilemmas was
the matter of what to do about Idris al-Senussi, who had been

promised much and expected more. Moreover, they had to find enough officers who could speak Arabic well who were also in tune with Arab culture and sensitivities. All this and there was 'a war on', as the saying goes, which meant that Cyrenaica would remain strategically important for a long time.

What were the long-term aims of Duncan Cumming and his senior staff and of the Arabists in the British Foreign Office? There are some learned critics who argue that the British intended to find and bolster 'a client monarch who would agree to satisfy their strategic interests and act as a break on threatening pressure from extreme elements' and that monarch was to be Emir Idris al-Senussi – or Sayyid Idris al-Senussi as he was then referred to so as not to reveal the cunning plan. The evidence for this comes from a book written by a sometime member of the British Military Administration, F. M. de Candole, which was privately published in 1990. There may have been some speculation of this nature but we must also remember that Egypt had designs on Cyrenaica and is displaying an interest as these words are being written. Italy was also likely to make a claim should Mussolini fall from power. It is easy to see that Libya's present condition has some precedent in its recent history.

How did Cumming solve the recruiting problem? He found twenty-seven Arabic-speaking British officers with experience enough to undertake the work but complained that many did not fill the job description adequately. For his leading officers he sought Arabists – as he understood the word – and, in particular, men who had been in the Sudan Political Service. He had served in that elite service himself and he was to adapt its methods when he took over.

The key question was what could these men offer which he needed? The answer is simple and it is known as Indirect Rule. In 1900 Fredrick Lugard, later Sir Fredrick Lugard, took charge of the large British Protectorate of Northern Nigeria. His domain covered an eye-watering 350,000 square miles and was hitherto ruled by Muslim sultans and emirs. His budget was small, as was his staff. He responded to the challenge by installing a British Resident at each of the Muslim courts and augmented them with subsidies to emirs and chiefs and kept things lively with the occasional 'punitive expedition'. He expected the British Residents to be the power behind the throne and never the throne itself. In hindsight we can see the downsides to this expediency. It stopped progress in its tracks by perpetuating existing hierarchies resistant to change and the Muslim sultans and emirs owed their loyalty to the infidel foreigner and so lost prestige and thus legitimacy.

In the Anglo-Egyptian Sudan the British faced a similar problem. They were ruling in tandem with the Egyptians who for their part were not pedalling very hard. The Sudan was a large country with a Muslim, Arab-speaking north and animist south. (It has recently separated along similar lines into two countries.) The British responded by introducing indirect rule and by recruiting high-flying personnel for this purpose to the Sudan Political Service.

Cumming and his staff arrived in Cyrenaica soon after 13 November 1942 and set up a temporary headquarters in the Green Mountains as Benghazi was severely damaged. The Italian farmers had abandoned the 1,800 or so farmsteads and thus imaginative ways of returning them to production were invented. Damaged tanks were modified into tractors for example and somehow many acres of good ground were cultivated. Food still had to be sourced and distributed. He formed a Cyrenaican Defence Force from veterans of the Libyan Arab Force. He was faced with few staff and a lot of territory to rule. His experience came into play. Crucially for Libya today, he set about the business of indirect rule by which means he politicised the Senussi sect by co-opting the restored Senussi Lodges among the tribes as centres of local government and thus launched the process which propelled Idris al-Senussi into power.

What happened to Tripolitania after Italy surrendered? It was different of course. No doubt some Italians left but some 40,000 remained. They were encouraged to stay and their property was protected. The British Military Administration of Tripolitania was run separately from Cyrenaica. Only 30 per cent of the population were Senussi followers and it was assumed that the Senussi Declaration did not therefore apply so it could operate within the international rules and regulations. Italian utilities, businesses, farms, vineyards, fisheries and more continued to function. It took some time before peoples stopped greeting each other with the fascist salute.

It is too easy to focus on Libya's northern cities. Now, the great majority of its people live there. The south-western province known as the Fezzan is still sparsely populated and is still home to Arab tribes with connections in the Sahel. Its western border with Algeria divides a Tuareg confederacy the majority of which live in Algeria. The Tuaregs are a colourful and often warlike people who range the central and southern Sahara. They are called the People of the Veil because their menfolk cover their faces at all times, even while eating. Their women are, in contrast to Arab and Berber women, unveiled. The Tuareg will appear again so we need to take them into account now. There are also a number of Tebu, another people without frontiers. They are kinfolk of the Teda who inhabit the remote and forbidding Tibesti Mountains in Chad. They are numerous in the oasis towns of Libya's Fezzan and were, and are, able to navigate the Badlands – a talent that makes them useful in war and people trafficking today. They have a fearsome reputation and they will also reappear in Haftar's story. The origins of the Tuareg and the Tebu are obscure.

It is the Fezzan which was freed of the few Italian troops defending it in December 1942 by a remarkably ramshackle band of Free French soldiers led by a colourful and aristocratic Free

French officer, Philippe, Comte de Hauteclocqe, whose *nom de guerre* was Leclerc. The French now began to assert a claim to post-war Fezzan, as though there were not enough claims on a land belonging to inhabitants whose war it was not. The French set up a military form of administration and did not encourage political activity. Though they were diligent in stimulating the economy, their tendency to be dictatorial was resented. French troop commanders acted in both military and civil capacities, as they did in the Algerian Sahara. In the west of the Fezzan, Ghat was attached to the French military region of southern Algeria and Ghadames to the French command of southern Tunisia. This troubled Libyan nationalists who feared that the French might claim the Fezzan, which they had coveted since the early nineteenth century when their North African empire was expanding. The French retained control of the Fezzan until Libya gained its independence in 1951 and they maintained a small military presence there until at least 1958.

The United Nations Cobbles Together a Nation Called Libya

There now began a protracted period of tortuous negotiations about post-war Libya. Why do we need to follow them? Because the glue applied to stick Libya together may not have lasted. We need to plod through some examples so that we can understand the rivalries at the heart of the present civil war.

The Great Powers visited the matter at the Potsdam Conference in 1945. By this time the USA was extending her strategic reach to counter the USSR. She now recognised the importance of the Libyan ports and airfields to her interests in the Mediterranean. This put a new emphasis on Libya's future with the USA, now a major player.

The effort to reach a solution to the Libya problem was handed over to the United Nations General Assembly in September 1948.

Thereafter, the pressures of the Cold War created differences which made for more delay. France and Britain were notably reluctant to reach agreement. The Big Four Council of Foreign Ministers sent a mission to Libya to gauge the aspirations of the people not before time it must be said. Early in 1948, after three months of work on the ground, the mission concluded that there was an overwhelming desire for independence. Despite a Russian suggestion that the French and British Military Governments should leave immediately, the commission made it clear that Libya was too impoverished economically, educationally, socially and politically for self-government.

Britain and Italy made another attempt to break the deadlock in 1949. Their respective foreign ministers, Ernest Bevin and Count Sforza, proposed that Britain should assume the trusteeship of Cyrenaica, Italy of Tripolitania and France the Fezzan. The trusteeships were to last for ten years, when Libya would seek UN approval for independence. The Bevin–Sforza plan failed because the Libyans were not prepared to accept Italian rule and demonstrated against it on the streets of Tripoli and Benghazi with more than usual energy, secretly egged on by the USSR and Egypt. For the first time, the Libyan National Congress Party emerged. It made its views clear and a consensus was reached in favour of independence.

The British now played a trump card. They unilaterally granted internal self-government to Cyrenaica, with Sayyid Idris as emir. When he had made a brief visit in 1944, he had been given a rousing welcome. However, he had refused to return for good from exile in Egypt until the British had completely relinquished control. This gave Sayyid Idris a dominant role in the negotiations about Libya's future and neatly protected British interests.

The United Nations, somewhat constrained by the British move in Cyrenaica, now began to make plans for independence. It remained to be decided if the provinces would go their separate ways as they threaten to do today. Somehow an agreement was cobbled together. The United Nations General Assembly, at its 250th plenary meeting on 21 November 1949, resolved that Libya would become 'an independent and sovereign State ... as soon as possible and not later than January 1, 1952, and that a constitution for Libya, including the form of the government, be determined by representatives of the inhabitants of Cyrenaica, Tripolitania, and the Fezzan, meeting and consulting together in a national assembly'.[3] This was to be the United Nations' first attempt to set up a sovereign state and there was some anxiety and a great deal of horse trading around at the time.

On 25 July 1950, the UN's Commissioner, Adrian Pelt, invited twenty-one prominent Arabs – seven each from Cyrenaica and the Fezzan, six from Tripolitania, and one representing the nation's minorities – to form a committee to discuss the composition of a National Assembly and how to select its members. The committee decided that it should consist of twenty members from each of the three territories, to be appointed by the chiefs of the territories. Once established the new National Assembly began drafting a constitution and making plans for a general election.

The discussions inevitably focused for some time on whether Libya should be a unified or a federal state. The possibility that one province would dominate a unitary government was a stumbling block not easily overcome. Gradually a compromise emerged, in which the Emir of Cyrenaica was to be invited to take the throne of a United Kingdom of Libya.

Thus it was that, in December 1950, the UN Assembly passed a resolution proposing that the three provinces – the Fezzan, Tripolitania and Cyrenaica – should be combined under the crown of Sayyid Mohammad Idris el Mahdi el Senussi, Emir

---

3. UN resolution quoted in Wechsberg, Joseph, 'Letter from Libya', *New Yorker*, 10 November 1951

of Cyrenaica. However, the compromises buried within this resolution were to rise again in 2011.

Was King Idris fit to lead a fractious, impoverished nation? Duncan Cumming, who knew him well, will have hoped that he might rally the people and find a source of income to keep it afloat but I know he had reservations. The new king was old and had always been a hypochondriac. He was heavily dependent on the British and US bases for revenue at first but Libya was sitting on great oil reserves. That brought the oil barons and oil rigs and great wealth. Could he handle the transformation from one of the world's poorest nations to one of its richest? And what of Khalifa Haftar as Ghaddafi arrived, making sweeping changes?

3

KING IDRIS AND A
CHANGING LIBYA

In 1969 the Red Castle in Tripoli stood, as it had for some 400 years, next to the Arch of Marcus Aurelius. It was a stark reminder of the city's Roman roots. The castle was where the Knights of St John and the Norman kings of Sicily briefly ruled, and where Ottoman pashas had kept their harems and dispatched their disreputable corsairs to prey on the merchant ships of the young USA. In the depths of the castle, the defiant graffiti of the captives of the Ottoman Turks could – and can still – be seen scratched into the walls. There is no trace, however, of the slaves who survived the journey across the Sahara to be sold in markets for shipping across the Mediterranean, much like migrants still are today.

The change in Libya in the late 1950s was subtle. The new colonial Italians, those who had ventured across the Mediterranean to settle where their Roman ancestors had once ruled, remained for a good while and the fashionable clothes shops, jewellers, hairdressers, cafes and restaurants still lived on. On Sundays, Italian families attended the late morning service in the cathedral and strolled past the cafes in their Sunday best greeting friends and being seen. The efficient municipal trash collections and the numerous police guarded the public from vermin and crime, but tin shacks were appearing on the fringes of the city as Libyans migrated into town in the hope of work in the decade-old oil bonanza. They were infiltrating the city as the first wave of true Libyans who had come to be ruled by Muammar Ghaddafi, whose image would dominate the Red Castle.

The British military presence was palpable. There was an infantry regiment in residence, a Royal Air Force station shared the civil airport and a Royal Tank Regiment occupied a barracks in the town of Homs. From time to time British troops and airmen appeared from elsewhere and honed their desert fighting skills in training areas or their low-level bombing techniques over ranges in the tribal hinterland. Not far out of town the USAF guarded their Wheelus Field where their undoubted air power could be heard and seen. In Benghazi there was another British military presence, smaller but similar to that in Tripoli, and in the remote east, near Tobruk, the RAF maintained a sizeable presence at El Adem.

This apparently excessive military hardware and soldiery had a cause. Until it became oil-rich, Libya had little value other than its strategic position. The subsidies and economic help Britain and the US paid and gave to the new Libya were essential but increasingly hard for the king to defend in the face of growing opposition and anti-Israeli fervour.

There was one event which had a lasting effect on Libya but which received little attention at the time. Nasser sent one of his close associates, Major General Ahmed Hassan el Faki, as the Egyptian Ambassador to Libya. El Faki arranged for over 500 Egyptian teachers to work in Libya, drawing salaries from Egypt as well as Libya itself. He also arranged for army personnel from Egypt to be seconded to the Libyan Army, including a senior officer. Alongside the Voice of the Arabs radio station, these teachers were to have a notable effect on young Libyan minds, not least on the young Muammar Ghaddafi.

King Idris was a holy man and neither warlike nor charismatic. Called the Shepherd King by some, he had passed much of his life in his remote oasis strongholds in the Libyan Desert from which he was evicted by the Italians. He was revered by his followers, who endowed him with near-saintly powers. But the mechanics of modern power were alien to him.

Tripoli boasted an ornate Italianate palace, but King Idris preferred to live in his modest palace in Tobruk. Perhaps he felt safe there. He was close to the RAF staging post at El Adem and there were RAF personnel in town. He was also near Jaghbub, where the mausoleum of his revered ancestor was preserved. He was surrounded by the large and loyal al-Abaidat tribe and within striking distance of the lordliest of the Sa'adi tribes. He favoured them and they protected him.

Personal security was among Idris's first considerations, especially as so much power was vested in him as monarch. The wider issues which were papered over during the rush to independence were still alive. Inter-tribal strife was always likely. The powerful, ambitious tribal leaders and sheiks to whom he had promised so much required management. The Berbers, especially those in the Western Mountains, were clamouring for a hearing. The Tuaregs and the Tebu were small but demanding minorities who occupied a lot of territory in the remote south.

Unsurprisingly, Idris did not trust his army. He was all too aware that senior army officers get ambitious and use their regiments to seize power. His regular army was unreliable, being recruited as it was from fractious tribes. History tells us he was right, for among its officers were Ghaddafi and his fellow plotters. Controlling Libya's long, inhospitable and truly remote southern border was – and is – also a challenge, and in 1969 there was a foreign policy to consider. It was not just the west – the Italians, the British and the French – who dominated Libya's story. When we look at its foreign policy from King Idris's (or Khalifa Haftar's) perspective we need to turn our minds towards the Sahel, that is the countries where the Libyan Desert and the Sahara encroach on the northern outliers of Equatorial Africa.

What were Idris's available resources when he assumed power? What were his strengths and weaknesses? The population was small. His army was ill equipped to project his power over great distances. There were few Libyans trained to lead. He knew he must prioritise personal and internal security, so he divided his forces into a regular army and a variety of armed police forces. He raised the Cyrenaican Defence Force (CDF) from officers of the old Libyan Arab Force who were members of the seven Sa'adi tribes of Cyrenaica and recruited from their own tribesmen. The CDF was trained by British Army personnel and was, in effect, a hybrid between a police force and an army. It was often referred to as the King's Pretorian Guard, accurately so it seemed to me. I remember it would parade once a year along the Benghazi Corniche past my office, in good marching order but with little military hardware.

The police force was numerous. There were two entities, the elite Federal Police and the local police who patrolled the towns and sometimes the hinterland. They eventually ranged from several lightly armed territorial forces to the mobile National Security Force equipped with helicopters and armoured cars. Units of the prestigious CDF, assisted and advised by British military specialists, were garrisoned at several places in Cyrenaica. The primary mission of the armed police was to counterbalance dissidents within the faction-torn armed forces and thus preclude a coup against the monarchy.

Idris established the Royal Libyan Military Academy in 1957 to train officers and with substantial British help his army slowly grew. By September 1969, its strength was around 6,500. That was near enough half the size of the CDF and the various police forces.

Idris kept his armed forces in hand by using them as a form of patronage, promoting officers from powerful tribes and families and moving them around from post to post to prevent them subverting their troops to serve their political ambitions. He declined to supply the army with tanks, artillery, and armoured personnel carriers which they might use against him as easily as they could against a hostile enemy.

By 1969 the king was old and tired and he truly looked it. To my knowledge he had attempted to abdicate at least once before and was dissuaded by his divan with the aid of a tribal demonstration of support. His dilemma was now serious. We cannot know for sure, but he was possibly clear sighted enough to see that the crown prince, Hassan al-Senussi, was not capable of replacing him and had realised that his favourite, Omar Shelhi, was tainted by corruption. Idris may have known that there was an army coup in the offing, possibly from Azziz Shelhi, the army chief of staff. Perhaps he decided to pre-empt him.

Abdication

Whether Idris knew about an impending coup or not, in August 1969, the king decided to take himself off to a spa in Turkey for medical treatment and a rest. He was by this time determined to abdicate and hoped to retire to the summer palace in Tobruk. He called his prime minister and the head of the senate to Turkey and handed them the instrument of abdication, naming the crown prince as his successor. It was to take effect on 1 September 1969. This is from the letter of abdication of King Idris, dated 4 August 1969:

> Most men's work is not completely devoid of imperfections, and when some years ago I felt weak. I offered my resignation, but you returned it. I obeyed your wish and withdrew it. Now,

due to my advanced years and weak body I find myself obliged to say for the second time that I am unable to carry this heavy responsibility.

There were a number of interested parties, most of whom were also sure there would be a coup. The Americans were watchful because their oil companies were heavily committed and their base at Wheelus was still important for their strategic plans. The CIA was represented in Libya at the time and it is strange that it could have had no knowledge of the various plotters. The Americans may have assumed that the British diplomats were au courant with the possible plotters and might be relied on to arrange for the Royal Enniskillen Fusiliers, who were stationed just outside Benghazi at the time, to intervene if the wrong coup took place. Both the British and the Americans were anxious to keep Nasser's hands off the oilfields.

I suspect that Nasser's men in Libya were confident that the outcome would be in their favour. One aspect which may have some relevance is that Nasser was himself ill and tired by now. His revolution had almost run its course in Egypt and his personal grip on events was loosening.

Ghaddafi's Putsch

However, the arrangement was forestalled by the young army officers surrounding Muammar Ghaddafi who were to assume power on behalf of the people.

The King was left high and dry in Turkey with no money to pay his hotel bills, which the Turkish government kindly settled. He went to Egypt and died in 1983. He is buried in Medina, Saudi Arabia. His government in Libya had achieved success in a number of fields, notably in education, for which it has received little recognition. The country he took over lacked expertise and infrastructure. He was at first forced to rely on the British and

American military bases and aid as a source of income. He also needed Western technology and expertise to find and exploit the oil beneath the desert, but his government had handled the oil companies wisely and well.

He had for some time wished to relinquish the burden of kingship and the great powers which had been thrust upon him were exercised by a small group of people who let him down in the end. The formation of the state of Israel and then an unwise decision by the British to go to war against Egypt over the Suez Canal had raised a revolutionary fervour among some young Libyans.

In short, Ghaddafi had seized power during a period of unusual unrest in Libya, caused by events outside the country, which he was able to exploit by developing a national paranoia directed against the British, the USA and Israel. His coup was bloodless because he was the quickest to act during the power vacuum left by the departure and abdication of King Idris. Or perhaps the young revolutionaries came to power so easily because the army was not sure who was leading it.

Either way, the immediate seat of power in the few days that followed the coup lay in the self-proclaimed Revolutionary Command Council, an echo of that which Nasser had created in Egypt after his coup. The RCC immediately declared that Libya was now a republic, warned other revolutionaries off with dire threats and attempted to assure foreign governments of their legitimacy.

A crucial event that did not happen was the intervention of the paramilitary Cyrenaican Defence Force. Perhaps Ghaddafi won them over – after all, they were close to the king and, like him, may have realised that there was no advantage in opposing the coup.

There was a pause while the Revolutionary Command Council consolidated its hold by putting the crown prince under house arrest and, also, arresting some senior army officers and government officials who might have opposed it.

On 7 September 1969, the day that the USA officially recognised the new Libyan leadership, the RCC announced that it had appointed a government. American-educated technician and long-term political prisoner Mahmud Sulayman al-Maghrabi would be prime minister. A council of eight ministers was also appointed, of whom two were military officers. The council was instructed to implement the state's general policy, as drawn up by the RCC. On 8 September the RCC promoted Captain Muammar al-Ghaddafi to the rank of colonel and appointed him commander-in-chief of the Libyan armed forces.

The ease with which a group of junior army officers succeeded in their coup still arouses questions in those quarters where accusations of American or British connivance stem from anti-Western sentiment. Why did Britain not intervene? It is clear that the British expected a coup and were prepared to make the best of it when it came. It had been the British policy to train the Libyan army and cosset it with support from the British Military Mission in the hope that a military coup would rebound in their favour. Though they had the warnings of Ted Lough on file, they had not expected Ghaddafi to prevail over the king's favourite, Azziz Shelhi, nor had the Egyptians who had also cultivated Shelhi's favour.

Did Britain support Ghaddafi's coup? It is most unlikely. While in Libya I was required to meet a number of British government ministers who passed through Idris and Benina airports on their way to sell arms or negotiate an orderly withdrawal from a colony. One was on his way to Aden, from whence the British were withdrawing after some unpleasant events. The minister and his team were positively unimpressive, another sign that Britain was rolling up her empire. The loss of India, the Malayan troubles, the Suez debacle, the Mau Mau in Kenya, the rebels in the Radfan in the heartland of Aden, EOKA in Cyprus and more of the same had accumulated to sap the British self-belief and reduce the support for imperialist adventures.

A sad little home-bound trickle of retiring British colonial governors passing through the Libyan airports was followed by a flush of new heads of state bound for the United Nations in New York or to meet Queen Elizabeth II in London. Presidents of newly independent countries, such as Jomo Kenyatta of Kenya, Kwame Nkrumah of Ghana and Dom Mintoff of Malta required my attendance as they stretched legs while their aircraft refuelled. The old order was changing at an ever-increasing rate.

Some of the new heads of state had been imprisoned by the British at one time or other in their careers or had led long struggles for independence, or both. That was not the case in Libya. However, the new regime presented itself as revolutionary and, in common with others of that ilk, needed an enemy to confront. It was to find one in the unwitting British.

It was soon clear that the British hope of gaining influence by training the Libyan army was a misjudgement. The trainees learnt quickly that power came out of the barrel of a gun. Some of the military coups which took place in the rapidly deflating British Empire were led by men trained in British military schools and staff colleges, but their regimes had no intention of accepting British influence. This was the case in Libya.

The British Labour politician Denis Healey was the Minister of Defence between 1964 and 1970. He visited Libya in that capacity to sell arms to the government of King Idris. His recollections about Ghaddafi's coup are interesting:

> I also paid several visits to Libya … It was obvious that the monarchy was about to fall at any moment to an army coup, and I tried to guess which of the young colonels I met was most likely to lead it. I decided it would probably be Colonel Shelhi … I was wrong.

He also wrote:

> I was told by our Ambassador that Shelhi had been woken by his batman on the morning of the coup with the words: 'Excuse me sir, the Revolution has begun.' 'Don't be silly,' was the reply. 'It's tomorrow.'[4]

As to the possibility of American connivance in the coup, I have no real insights, but their embassy in Libya was between ambassadors at the time. The upshot is that it is likely that all parties expected a military coup. They decided to make the best of it and to wait and see how the Revolutionary Command Council played its hand. But Ted Lough apart, no diplomat or MI6 or CIA agent predicted the Ghaddafi personality cult which was to come.

Ghaddafi's Personality Cult

Early misgivings may have surfaced when the Revolutionary Command Council asserted that engaging in political activity was treasonable. It added that the RCC was the highest authority in the Libyan Arab Republic and that it was unchallengeable. Trade unions were made illegal and supporters of King Idris and his regime were tried in courts presided over by RCC members. There were also some puritanical measures, such as closing the nightclubs where female dancing troupes were employed to make conversation with male guests, and banning the sale of alcoholic beverages. The latter created a thriving private home-brewing culture among expatriate workers.

As the reins tightened, there came at least two attempts to bring the regime down. One was said to have been initiated by

---

4. Healey, Denis, *The Time of My Life* (London: Michael Joseph, 1989), p. 322

Omar Shelhi, now in exile, who attempted to hire a company called Watch Guard, a group of British mercenary soldiers run by David Stirling, the British war hero and founder of the SAS. The idea was that ex-SAS men should raid Tripoli and release a number of political prisoners, including Azziz el Shelhi, from the notoriously awful gaol known cynically as the Tripoli Hilton. The British mercenaries were then to withdraw and leave the prisoners, and others, to mount a counter-coup. The operation has been described in detail in *The Hilton Assignment* by Patrick Seale. It appeared that some of David Sterling's associates were convinced that the counter-coup would succeed. I suspect that their optimism was ill founded. That Stirling was quietly warned off is sometimes cited to prove that Ghaddafi was supported by the British. It is more likely that the British government did not wish to deal with the diplomatic fallout from a counter-coup financed by Omar Shelhi and involving a prominent war hero, especially as it was unlikely to succeed.

The second, over-ambitious, attempted counter-coup was planned by a relative of King Idris, Prince Abdulla Abed, a colourful personage known as the Black Prince. He was said to have funded a force of mercenaries recruited in Chad with the intention of ousting Ghaddafi, but the French got wind of it and managed to alert the RCC. The French were later to make some spectacular armaments deals with the Ghaddafi regime.

With few opposers, the Libyan Revolutionary Command Council began to develop a personality cult around Ghaddafi and to strengthen their hand in Libya with a series of gestures. They seem to have concluded that oil revenues were sufficient to compensate for the loss of aid and rents received for the US and British military bases. They also gambled that Britain and the US would acquiesce to the early removal of their military, providing they continued to receive favourable treatment for their oil companies.

Ghaddafi now made a number of public speeches and staged events which led the Libyan people to believe that he was confronting the imperialist enemies by removing them. The gestures were mainly for a Libyan audience because both Britain and the USA readily agreed to relinquish their bases by early 1970, but Ghaddafi made sure that he was seen as an anti-imperialist hero by declaring the anniversaries of their evacuations as public holidays. Ghaddafi's image now dominated the Red Castle and he would tell his female conquests, 'I am Libya.'

Ghaddafi struck two further blows against the British by nationalising Barclays Dominion, Colonial and Overseas Bank and, as we have seen, cancelling arms contacts of some considerable value made by the previous regime with British companies.

Ghaddafi had learnt a lesson in brinkmanship from Nasser, who had defied British might by nationalising the Suez Canal, and he now applied it when dealing with the oil companies. He set out to break the hold of the Seven Sisters' cartel and assert the sovereignty of Libya over its own oil. In doing so, he changed the geopolitics of oil forever. This was an achievement of considerable importance to other oil producers, but also had the effect of greatly increasing the price of oil worldwide.

Military Expansion

To the growing consternation of the British and the US, Ghaddafi now turned to Russia, which was, and remains, eager to perch on NATO's southern flank. He purchased enormous quantities of military hardware – some authorities have suggested that between 1973 and 1983 Libya spent $28 billion on new armaments. It seems that $20 billion went to the USSR and the Soviet bloc. Libya was said to have 3,000 tanks, making it probably the eighth-largest such force in the world at the time. The Libyan army's range of tracked and wheeled armoured vehicles gave it the capacity to deploy readily over long distances. Rocket systems, engineering equipment, infantry weapons, fire control systems, flame throwers and anti-tank guided missiles were in ample supply.

By 2002, the best assessment suggested that the Libyan Army made up about two-thirds of the armed forces at 45,000 men, of whom 25,000 were believed to be conscripts. At the same time the Libyan Air Force consisted of around 10,000 men and the main air bases were Uqba ibn Nafi (the old USAF base previously called Wheelus) near Tripoli, and Jamal al-Nasser at Benina near Benghazi. The base at Hun, an oasis where Ghaddafi's tribe had holdings, were expanded. There were also bases at Kufra, Jabal Unwainat, Sebha and Tobruk. The air-defence units were armed with ground-to-air missiles which were based in five defence regions at the military airfields.

The navy was said to have a nominal role of 6,500 men and its two frigates, three corvettes, numerous speedboats and four submarines were based in Tripoli, Benghazi, Tobruk, Khums, Marsa Brega and Ras Hilal.

However accurate the figures given for Libyan military purchases may be, there can be no doubt that Ghaddafi gave priority to the procurement of arms and military materiel over domestic spending. For a long time, arms imports represented over half the total defence expenditures. His problems lay in the sophisticated nature of the armaments and the technology needed to support them. It has been estimated that more than half the equipment he purchased was stored, or unserviceable. This was especially so for the Libyan Air Force, which had been struggling to develop trained air and ground crews to match the acquisition of modern planes and weaponry. It has also been said that Libyan air units were reluctant to commit themselves and did not perform well in air-to-air combat.

The Rise of Haftar

Where was Khalifa Haftar during and after Ghaddafi's putsch? When he graduated from the Royal Military Academy he was commissioned as an artillery officer. He appears to have been assigned to deter the USAF from scrambling aircraft from Wheelus Field to attack Ghaddafi's forces, presumably by deploying whatever anti-aircraft weaponry was available to him. He was promoted to captain after the 1969 revolution and went to Egypt to observe and attend staff college.

Haftar's tribal connections did not threaten Ghaddafi, a consideration which was to grow in importance as power shifted away from the Sa'adi tribes towards the Ghaddadfa and its allies such as the Warfella and the Awlad Suleiman.

Introspection can be a dangerous tool for it plays havoc with objectivity and objectivity is sorely needed when discussing the motivation of military leaders. For Khalifa Haftar, a man not given to talk about such things, the events in Ouadi Doum in Chad were to result in a military defeat, betrayal by his sometime leader, years as a prisoner of war, adoption as part of Ronald Reagan's proxy war on Ghaddafi and exile in the USA – events which must surely have focussed his mind if not supplied him with some considerable motivation. Haftar's ability to survive such a turbulent period says much for the tenacity and force of his character.

Among the characters involved in this colourful story are Ronald Reagan, for whom little introduction is needed; Hissene Habré, a Tebu who became president of Chad between 1982 and 1990 and was later charged with crimes against humanity; and Goukouni Oueddei, who was head of state for Chad from 1979 to 1982 and whose sister married one of Ghaddafi's colonels. There were also some publicity-shy CIA agents in the mix, along with Hassan Djamous, a much-underrated soldier, sometimes compared to Erwin Rommel, who was later murdered in a power struggle. This cast of characters and many Haftar was to meet later, such as President Putin, lift his life story somewhat out of the ordinary.

As for Haftar himself, how had he fared under Ghaddafi's unpredictable command as he pursued his army career? From news reports and his own claims, it seems that he commanded the Libyan contingent during the 1973 Arab–Israeli War and participated in crossing the Suez Canal. He was later appointed artillery commander in Tripoli.

In 1975, he was appointed commander of Tobruk's defences, and between 1976 and 1978 he commanded Libya's air-defence system. After Ghaddafi purged the armed forces, he was assigned to insignificant units for three years and in 1978 he was sent to the Soviet Union to complete a general staff course at the Vesterel Military Academy. A search of the available data, though not his official army records, tell us that he was later to return to the USSR for a general leadership course at the M.V. Frunze Military Academy.

Some sources suggest that Haftar may have tried to resign from the army in 1974 and again in 1976, perhaps implying that he was already restive about Ghaddafi's idiosyncratic leadership.

Haftar was commander of the city of Tobruk from 1981 to 1986 and it is possible he was among the first people to go to the assistance of Ghaddafi after President Reagan's controversial bombing raid on his Bab al-Aziziya barracks in Tripoli in April 1986. That year he was identified in Benghazi, where his brother was a prominent citizen, as the colonel commanding the whole eastern region.

The Invasion of Chad

Even so, according to Haftar, he took command of the manoeuvres in Libya's south-east – possibly in 1978 but more likely in 1980 – and was in still in charge when Ghaddafi turned his sights to Chad.

Promoted that year to colonel, his highest rank under Ghaddafi, he remained in Chad until 1981. Personnel records are hard to come by under present circumstances but we know from a few journalists that at one time or another there were four colonels commanding the Libyan army occupying the North of Chad. They were – though probably not in the right order – Haftar himself; Masoud Abdul Hafiz al-Ghaddafi, who was a member of Muhammar Ghaddafi's tribe; the air force colonel Ali Sharif al-Rifi; and the most colourful of them, the tall, cool Colonel Radwan with his British-style swagger stick and his belt loaded with bullets.

Chad is a large, landlocked country divided by religion, geography and ethnicity – fertile animist and Christian south and desert/mountainous Islamist north. A Sudanese war lord called Rabih az Zubayr conquered the three neighbouring Sahel kingdoms of Wadai, Bagurimi and Kanem-Bornu around 1893. He held them until the French defeated his army and established their colonial rule in 1913 over the three kingdoms and combined them into what is now Chad. For the French North African Empire of which it now became part, Chad had a unique position as it bridges sub-Saharan and North Africa and also the east and west Sahel. The French ruled there until 1960 when Chad became independent. In 1963, political parties were outlawed. That set off a guerrilla war in the Muslim north which the French, whose interest in Chad continues today, returned to sort out. For a time, Chad was stable. Until Ghaddafi declared an interest.

As we have seen, Ghaddafi had purchased unusually large quantities of arms and expanded his armed forces. He could do so because he had achieved unprecedented personal power. His first intention was to use his arsenal, his army and his money to recreate a modern version of the historic Arab caliphates and to destroy Israel in the process. He was rebuffed by his fellow Arab leaders, perhaps because of his personality and certainly because they were unwilling to sacrifice their own grip on power. So he turned his ambitions towards Africa. He befriended Uganda's leader, Idi Amin, the redoubtable and often ridiculed son of an executioner; he underpinned the regime of the old Marxist Robert Mugabe, with disastrous results for many Zimbabweans; he meddled in the affairs of the Sudan, Mali and Niger; and he supported the ANC, for which Nelson Mandela was the grateful beneficiary. Now he wanted Chad.

Ghaddafi invaded and occupied northern Chad. The project cost the Libyan people dear, but by this time he had bolstered his power over them by means of a ruthless secret service and the evisceration of civil society. It is hard to imagine the feelings of Libyan families in the winter of 1986 as they watched the execution of nine fundamental Islamists broadcast by state TV.

Chad's border with Libya, which the two countries disputed violently between 1973 and 1994, is a hostage to fortune. The border had been loosely defined, leaving a disputed ribbon of dry and desolate land called the Aouzou Strip which neither country could hope to control. Ghaddafi's interest in Chad was preceded by a long history of Libya hosting Chadian anti-government rebels who crossed freely into the South Libyan Desert.

In 1973, Libyan forces moved into to the Aouzou Strip and built an airfield. It was to become the advance base for increasing Libyan military intervention. Ghaddafi's subsequent unrestrained incursion into, and sometimes occupation of, northern Chad between 1973 and 1987 should be counted among the better logistical performances in modern military history. But while it stands out as grandiose, it was very costly in terms of life and treasure.

Ghaddafi had seven C-130H Hercules transports flown mainly by British and other European mercenary pilots, some of whom were old friends of Edwin Wilson, the convicted ex-CIA Ghaddafi supplier. These planes were supplemented by six Soviet-supplied Ilyushin 76 freighters and some Italian G-222 transports. The logistics base at Ouadi Doum was at the Chadian end of Ghaddafi's air bridge. It not only had storage facilities but the means of handling and servicing the aircraft. It was in this flat, hot desert that Khalifa Haftar found himself in early 1987. He had been given the title of Operational Group East Commander, but he was later to imply that he had been posted there by Muammar Ghaddafi because he had become too popular. Popularity had proved a threat to Ghaddafi in the past, such as in 1973 when there was an attempted coup by RCC member Omar Meheishi supported by some army units. Meheishi was killed and nearly 200 army officers believed to have been involved were arrested.

At the Ouadi Doum base, around 3,000 personnel were accommodated in portable huts and what the Americans call trailers fitted with window-mounted air-conditioners. An irrigation system piped water to a vegetable garden which we can be sure grew plenty of hot peppers, of which the Libyans are notably fond. The garden was the only greenery to be found for hundreds of miles.

Good logistics and effective civil engineering were evident. Underground storage areas were dispersed throughout the base, each capable of storing twelve T-62 tanks protected from sand damage, prying eyes and aerial attack. In storage and in use were SA-6 anti-aircraft missiles and armed personnel carriers, all of Soviet manufacture. There was a 3,000-metre runway able to support heavy transport aircraft, fixed-wing and helicopter fighting aircraft were dispersed around the airfield, and fuel and explosives were supplied and stored safely. The base was protected by wire and landmines. The setup was impressive. But there were some signs which would have alerted a skilled inspecting officer that morale was low. While they may sound petty to civilians, they are not. Ouadi Doum was isolated, blown sand is not a welcome substrate other than at seaside resorts and men without women for long are unhappy. There was clearly no barber available, and men spent too long with shaggy hair and in green fatigues. Why does all this matter? It is simple. Unhappy men fight badly.

For Haftar's part, it is easy to see that he was not as free as he would have liked in his role at Oudi Doum. We know he was micromanaged by Ghaddafi, who assumed command from Tripoli. Ghaddafi was inexperienced, inflexible and too far from the action. But perhaps more crucial was the mindset of the two leaders. Both Ghaddafi and Haftar – and, I suspect, the majority of Libyan military officers – believed that simply applying Soviet technology and tactics was the formula for military success. The need for good intelligence and resilience was not appreciated and overconfidence was perhaps a polite description of the prevailing military mindset. The example of their ancestors who savaged heavily armoured Italian units between Haftar's birthplace Ajdabiya and Marsa Brega in 1923 had clearly been forgotten. In the end, defeat came in a similar fashion.

That Ghaddafi was sometimes challenged at home by a coup is unsurprising. In retrospect, the peregrinations and adventures of Khalifa Haftar from a military disaster in Chad's Ouadi Doum to a home in the shadow of the CIA's HQ in Langley, Virginia are easier to understand if we view him in the light of the disaster at Ouadi Doum and the other humiliations visited on the Libyans in Chad.

For Haftar's story we can dismiss the history of much of the Libyan occupation of Chad for others to untangle with the words of John Wright: 'Libyans have fought and died and squandered their oil revenue (in Chad) on adventures for which they would be hard pressed to give a coherent or reasonable justification. Apart from the occupation of the Aozou strip in 1973, Tripoli's role seems to have been a series of reactions to perceived threats from within Chad or ill-considered attempts to seize opportunities for local or regional advantage.' He goes on to say that 'since 1969 Libyan foreign policy has largely reflected the ideals, visions and inconsistencies of Colonel Muammar Ghaddafi', Khalifa Haftar's motivation might well be reflected in these words.

The Tebu

Libya and Chad share a people without frontier: the Tebu. They have escaped the attention of much of the English-speaking world. They have not been a hospitable people and there are few who have written about them. The American anthropologist Cabot Briggs is among those few who have done so. In 1920, an unusual British woman, Rosita Forbes, made the journey from Ajdabiya to the then 'forbidden' oasis of Kufra by camel and lived to write about it. Like many successful women in those days she trailed a history of tittle-tattle but she was courageous and resourceful and described the Tebu and the terrain they inhabit in her book.

The Tebu have not, until very recently, owed allegiance to a state nor did they, until recently, have strong leaders. There are not many of them, probably around 200,000, though that is but a best estimate. They live in, and are psychologically and physically adapted to, a vast region of around 1.7 million square kilometres in the remote northern Chad where the Tibesti Mountains lie, part of South Libya, some of Niger in the west and, to the east, a little of Darfur in the Sudan. Under pressure from their traditional enemies from the north, they have shifted south a little, perhaps as far as Lake Chad. Their origin remains a mystery and probably reaches back a thousand years into antiquity.

Their language and their appearance set them apart. Their skin colour is very dark yet they have clear European traits. Their menfolk are able to navigate where others would be fatally lost and they range over great distances.

When travelling they appear to need little water and food and they were feared by all as raiders of slaving caravans or of innocent travellers. They are able to traverse great arid regions which they know as well as London cab drivers do their own perplexing city. They share this talent with a number of Bedouin tribes who have traded across the Sahara from time immemorial. They occupied Kufra until the late eighteenth century and some still live there today, dominated by the Arab Sway tribe. They also occupy some of the old slave-trading oases of the Fezzan such as Murzuq. Their westward neighbours in the Fezzan are their traditional enemies and competitors, the Tuaregs.

The two Chadian Tebu with roles in the developing problem between Ghaddafi and Chad were both war lords with political ambitions from the north. One was Goukouni Oueddei from the Tibesti and the other was Hissene Habré from Borku. Habré was a cruel, uncompromising guerrilla leader who would not negotiate with Libya. Oueddei was a realist and would. When Habré challenged Oueddei in 1980, the latter signed a treaty with Libya which legitimised the presence in northern Chad of around 7,000 regular Libyan Army personnel supported, but not well, by a similar number of Ghaddafi's Islamic Legion. The latter were often reluctant mercenaries who had little training or enthusiasm for their trade.

Then, at a crucial time for Haftar, Goukouni Oueddei fell out with Ghaddafi personally. He was said to have been wounded in a shootout in Tripoli in October 1987, leaving the Libyan forces in Chad without local guides and local intelligence, thus operationally handicapped in the testing terrain.

Habré's Chadian army was commanded by the thirty-year-old Hassan Djamous. His cloak work was guile and he would deliver his fatal sword thrusts from the back of Toyota trucks. Djamous is little known outside Chad but some have tried to compare him favourably with Erwin Rommel. His genius was to adapt the Tebu's tradecraft when brigandage was their way of life. They were masters of manoeuvre and perfected the lightning raid on large, ponderous camel caravans shuffling through their homelands. Djamous adapted these tactics with devastating effect on the conventionally armed Libyans, using Toyota half trucks instead of camels and fitting them with machine guns, automatic grenade launchers and Milan anti-tank guided missiles which could destroy Libyan armoured vehicles at a range of 1,800 meters. He used a combination of diversionary tactics and raids to demoralize and defeat Libyan troops. Columns of his armed Toyotas would appear in one direction, drawing the attention of the Libyans, then the main Chadian force would approach from the opposite direction and attack with missiles, destroying the unwieldy tanks and routing the poorly trained Libyans. (Ghaddafi's army was to face an another improvised 'army' of armed Toyotas in the Arab Spring of 2011 and fared badly, as we will see. Was his army in 2011 burdened by the same faults it had been in 1987?)

The ignominious end to Ghaddafi's ambitions in Chad was brought about by his own hubris. Khalifa Haftar, though he made two bad mistakes as a district commander, was micromanaged by Ghaddafi, who had lost an essential local ally, goaded the French with a bombing raid to establish air superiority over northern Chad and dismissed Haftar's advice. More to the point, as Hassan Djamous and his Toyota-mounted tribesmen went from success to success, so US aid to Chad increased. This was as much personal as political, as President Reagan became as obsessed with Muammar Ghaddafi as Anthony Eden had with Nasser.

Reagan and Ghaddafi

While Ghaddafi 'occupied' northern Chad, the Pentagon believed that Libyan troops stationed there, tenuously connected to Tripoli by a supply line that stretched thousands of miles, were an 'Achilles Heel' for Libya. They therefore represented a golden opportunity to 'bloody Ghaddafi's nose' and 'increase the flow of pine boxes back to Libya', in the reported words of US Secretary of State Alexander Haig. It was a particularly Western viewpoint as there were to be plenty of bodies and no pine boxes. The US now began to see Haftar as a potential asset which they could exploit against his erstwhile leader.

When making this assessment the Pentagon had the support of persuasive evidence. They could count at least two attempted military coups in 1975. In March, a considerable number of senior military officers failed to oust Ghaddafi. More dramatically, a coup in July by a number of his companions on the Revolutionary Command Council, including the commander of his personal guard, also failed. There is no evidence that Haftar was party to these and other plots but news of them was widespread in intelligence circles. How did Ghaddafi survive in power for more than forty years? Perhaps the strength of his security battalions, carefully recruited and trained and outside the army structure, should have been taken into account. They were largely commanded by Ghaddafi family members and were probably around 10,000 strong.

President Reagan's personal animosity towards Ghaddafi came into play in the events that followed. Reagan hoped that Ghaddafi's humiliation in Chad would precipitate his downfall in Libya and was ready to pay good money to help it happen.

The Chadians realised that Ghaddafi's strength lay in his ability to bomb their capital from Quadi Doum, Faya Largo and airfields in South Libya. They therefore opened their account with a raid on Libya's well-armed communications centre at Fada.

On 2 January 1987, Hassan Djamous struck with his trademark long-distance raid combined with surprise and speed. He is believed to have killed or otherwise disposed of 784 Libyans, ninety-two T-85 tanks and considerably more hardware. He lost eighteen soldiers and three armed Toyotas. He had done much to disrupt Ghaddafi's command and control. Some sources suggest that Hassan Djamous was supplementing his local knowledge with information received via the Washington High Speed Facsimile System from the US Defence Intelligence Agency, who were transmitting overhead satellite views about troop locations and movements. This is not impossible but needs corroboration which is not readily available.

The countdown to the battle of Ouadi Doum commenced in a brilliantly executed low-level raid on 16 February 1987 by the French air force, who successfully bombed and closed the runway at Ouadi Doum. Some say they hit the radar but there is confusion on that count.

Haftar and Ghaddafi exchanged views, it seems, about the recapture of the Libyan communication base at Fada. In the end Ghaddafi instructed Haftar to organise a fighting column of sufficient strength to do the job. Haftar must have done the staff work and dispatched the column which included numerous tanks, armoured personnel carriers and artillery. It got as far as a pass known as Bur Kora, 30 miles along the desert track. On 19 March the Chadians attacked here using their agile Toyota pickup trucks with anti-tank weapons to overcome the ponderous and surprised Libyans. Many Libyans were killed but some retreated in the direction of Ouadi Doum. Haftar sent a relief column which met the Chadian Toyotas about 12 miles along the road from their base and was badly mauled, with survivors retreating in disorder.

Djamous seems to have benefitted from some accurate intelligence while engaged in this operation, and Haftar must bear the blame for his failure to have the route reconnoitred. He may have lost the services of his sometime Chadian allies but he had plenty of aircraft at his disposal. While the column commander should have put out a reconnaissance screen, there is no excuse for Haftar's failure.

Did he have confidence in Ouadi Doum's defences? The outer defences were along a sand ridge about 1,000 yards from a minefield through which a narrow lane led to some strong points guarding the entrance. The lane and the strong points were designed to concentrate attackers into the field of defensive fire. On 22 March, an estimated 2,500 Chadians breached the sand ridge, braved the minefields, and fought their way past the strong points. Once they fell the Libyans capitulated. There was no further resistance. Some escaped, but many were captured. Among them was Colonel Haftar.

There followed a unique bombing campaign as the Libyan Air Force attempted to bomb the cornucopia of their own expensive weapons. They were unsuccessful, but they may have helped some Libyans to escape.

Hassan Djamous struck a terminal blow to Ghaddafi's military ambitions in Chad. On 5 September 1987, he led his 2,000 Toyota-borne troops into Libya and took the Maatan-al Sarra air base in the Kufra district, which 25,000 Libyans failed to defend. The panache and guile shown by Djamous surely puts him among the best practitioners of desert warfare. A ceasefire was agreed between Ghaddafi and Habré, by now the power in Chad, on 11 September.

Haftar is burdened with the failure at Ouadi Doum. Some see it as a professional failure and base their assessment of his military leadership on his performance on 22 March 1987. The loss of Maatan al-Sarra within Libya was a greater failure without the extenuating circumstances of Ouadi Doum. One key to the Ouadi Doum failure, and for that matter the spectacular victories of

Hassan Djamous which drove Ghaddafi's forces out of Chad, is to be found in the shootout in Tripoli in which Goukouni Oueddei was wounded. The war was changed fundamentally as a result.

Until 1978, the Libyans supplied the tanks, artillery and the air power. It was the Libyans' ability to bomb the Chadian capital, N'Djamena, that mattered most. Goukouni Oueddei's Chadians were the infantry and the scouts, and they did the fighting. In a pitched battle the Libyans could stand behind them and use their superior firepower to win. When Habré's fighters joined forces with Oueddei's, however, the Libyans were eyeless. They lost the first line of defence for their logistical bases, their communications base and the crucial engineering support for their aircraft.

There was a further and fundamental innovation which proved fatal. The Chadian Army, commanded brilliantly by Hassan Djamous, was now well trained, ruthless, mobile and provided with anti-tank and anti-aircraft weaponry which was both accurate and would fit on the back of a Toyota Hilux. The Libyans hadn't just lost their infantry; it had turned against them and gained the support of the USA.

When assessing Haftar's performance at Ouadi Doum some account of the competence of his contemporaries is needed. Sometime in 1962, a British officer in the British Military Administration asked me if it would be possible to source Halal-certified field rations because the Libyan army took a flock of sheep along when on manoeuvres. This limited its flexibility and increased its visibility. It would be too easy to be derisory about this. The issue of flexibility and military creativity is of fundamental importance in modern warfare. So is communication. They are not inherited; they must be learned.

Throughout my years of working with Libyans it was the impact of modern technology and its concomitant management techniques that I needed to mediate. The Libyan Army in Chad in 1978 was equipped with ample Soviet-manufactured military hardware and trained to use it by the book. However, the flexibility built into the Russian training manuals had not been assimilated by the young Libyan officers.

The need to be right despite evidence to the contrary was a burden that young Libyan males suffered from most acutely. It took them a long time to learn to adjust to inevitable mistakes in times of acute crises, to communicate them upwards along the command chain and to learn to avoid them in future.

These traits surfaced at Ouadi Doum and were recognisable in the performance of the Libyan army in combat before and afterwards – at Maatan al-Sarra, for example. They can be seen in the failure to reconnoitre, to plug gaps in defensive lines or even to shore up sectors under pressure, to counter-attack or to report setbacks upwards. There may have been failures at the strategic or even the political level but it was the failures at the tactical level, that is at the junior and middle-ranking officer level, which were the most critical during the last battles of the Libyan Army in Chad in 1978.

In sharp contrast, the spectacular successes of Djamous were achieved by adapting the Tebu traditional raiding techniques using Toyota pickups with modern and light weaponry. That they may have been supported by sophisticated intelligence gathering and communications as I suggest they were does not detract from the obvious lesson that al-Qaeda and the Islamic State has learned and applied in Libya and elsewhere. Has Khalifa Haftar also learned from Ouadi Doum?

Colonel Haftar, with an estimated 600 of his troops, fell into the hands of Hassan Djamous and his victorious tribesmen, who were unlikely to have heard of the Geneva Convention governing the treatment of prisoners of war. They were about to move into the world of Hissene Habré.

Habré had realised that Libyan POWs were useful bargaining chips in his geopolitical trade-offs. Many of them were held in his prison compounds until after his ruthless reign as President of Chad was terminated. He found that the longer he held on to them and the more he manipulated their image, the more valuable they became.

Habré permitted Ronald Reagan to build a force of Libyan POWs to challenge Ghaddafi, trained by American intelligence officials in sabotage and other guerrilla skills at a base near N'Djamena, the Chadian capital. Reagan's eagerness to topple Colonel Ghaddafi made the scheme attractive. We are about to follow its fortunes.

4

HAFTAR IN THE HEART OF DARKNESS

Betrayal in Chad

The Human Rights Watch reports that most of the Libyan prisoners of war in Chad were taken in 1987. 'In the first three months of that year,' the *New York Times* reported, 'an estimated 3,000 Libyans were killed, or wounded or deserted and 900 taken prisoner ... subsequent figures vary widely, up to 2,500.' The same Human Rights Watch paper states that 'after Idriss Déby took power on December 1st 1990, almost 500 had been returned home and between 500 and 600 to have been evacuated to the United States ... The number of men missing from this accounting allows for speculation that the last years of Hissène Habré's presidency witnessed the death of a large number his Libyan captives.'[5]

It soon became clear to Colonel Haftar and his fellow POWs that Ghaddafi had denied they existed. In a personal humiliation for Haftar he is said to have denied even knowing him, asking the

---

5. The numbers quoted here are from the Human Rights Watch paper 'Chad: The Victims of Hissene Habre Still Awaiting Justice'. They are partially corroborated by the research notes of the Washington Institute for Near East Policy compiled by Barak Barfi.

press something along the lines of 'Who is Khalifa Haftar? Some shepherd who has strayed into Chad?' In February 1987 he said, 'The information mentioning the concentration of Libyan troops in Chad – is lies.' He repeated the charge after the fall of Ouadi Doum. The Chadians broadcast Ghaddafi's speeches denying their existence and asserting the Libyans were 'mercenary gangs'.

Ghaddafi's reason for denying that there were Libyan POWs in Chad is unknown, but it is more than likely related to an agreement he had made with President Mitterrand of France as far back as September 1984, to evacuate his army of occupation from the border with Chad in concert with a French withdrawal. Needless to say, Ghaddafi did not comply with the agreement.

Ghaddafi's personal abandonment of Haftar made him his implacable enemy. But his denial that there were POWs at all had a wider political implication: it made it clear to Habré, who had few scruples about the Geneva Convention and international scrutiny, that if Libyans POWs did not exist officially, he was free to kill them. There is substantial evidence that he did just that.

There are few available eyewitnesses to the events and very few official documents in the public domain we can rely on to support the story of the Libyan POWs in Chad. There is also little by way of reliable evidence to go by in the well-guarded CIA archives, and Haftar himself still has to guard his history with care – even a little knowledge may serve his enemies during his present engagement in propaganda wars.

We do know that the Human Rights Watch quoted a report from *Africa Confidential* on 6 January 1989 saying:

The United States and Israel have constructed a series of bases in Chad, Cameroon and elsewhere in which they are training a substantial Contra force of Libyans, including up to 2,000 prisoners of war taken by the Chadian Army in 1987. The aim is to overthrow Colonel Muammar Ghaddafi ... The NFSL's

(National Front for the Salvation of Libya, i.e. the Contras) military instructors include both US nationals and Chadians trained in the USA ... Close to the NFSL's Ouadi Doum base is a stockpile of arms captured by Chadian armed forces during the 1987 battles and subsequently sold to the USA and France. The arsenal is now controlled by officials of the Central Intelligence Agency.

The implication is that the Chadians had concentrated their Libyan POWs in the Ouadi Doum base, which would make sense. Once the main defences of the Ouadi Doum base had been breached the Libyans had offered no further resistance. The base was hardly damaged. The Chadians were not numerous nor did they have facilities for the reception of POWs. The simple answer would be to leave the Libyans where they were, disarm them and put them to work, which corroborates the *Africa Confidential* report's suggestion that Ouadi Doum was the main POW camp. There were several eastern European mercenaries on the base who had been servicing the aircraft and military hardware, but they were shipped home as soon as it became diplomatically possible. So only the Libyans remained. Until Ghaddafi decided to acknowledge that they existed, they were in limbo. It was now up to Habré to decide their fate.

We need to adjust our minds and discipline our imagination to empathise with the Libyan captives in the base at Ouadi Doum. Long exposure to films and stories about the Second World War has given some of us a picture of heavily guarded borders which heroic POWs cross in peril, possibly on motorcycles. In reality, the Libyan POWs were a mixed group. If there were many pressed men from Pakistan in Ghaddafi's Islamic Legion, they will have been seriously discontented. There were certain to have been a number of conscripts who would also have been unhappy. The literacy level among regular soldiers was alarmingly low and we know that there were difficulties in Libya with conscription, unpopular in any case and particularly so when the Chadian wars were in progress. Add these issues to tribal allegiances, shortage of clothes and food, power breakdowns in the heat and the lack of women, and Haftar and his officers would have been hard pressed to contain their anger. Haftar himself would not have been popular, but he learned how to deal with it. When we read the stories which emerge about him at this time we must take the circumstances into account and recognise that morale was low even before his great defeat.

The problems for a Libyan POW who might decide to escape and make his way home were principally distance and inhospitable terrain. The Libyan tribes among whom the young Khalifa Haftar lived and to which his mother belonged, the Sway and the Magharba, had traded in Chad for many years and the Senussi were there in strength until the French expelled them. There were family connections, and Chad has its own Arab people, often overlooked even today. The Tebu people were not confined by arbitrary borders and since the great oil bonanza in Libya many Chadians had moved there to work on the oil rigs and terminals. Anti-Ghaddafi Libyans were in N'Djamena. One of them was Dr Mohmad Youssef Magariaf.

The Formation of the National Front for the Salvation of Libya

The Bedouin tent pitched in the highly fortified bastion that was once Bab al-Aziziya barracks in Tripoli was symbolic of Muammar Ghaddafi's tribal origin. It also demonstrated to those who cared to think about it the cultural isolation in which not just his origins but his personality had imprisoned him. The images of him that dominated the lives of Libyans over the years in which they endured his personality cult show him first as a slim young army officer dressed unostentatiously in British uniform but had by now descended into a theatrical, almost comic caricature. He had changed. When he led the putsch in 1969 he was first among equals of the Revolutionary Command Council. Now he became the isolate whose control over what his people heard and watched and what they talked about stultified their intellectual, religious and political life. He withdrew into the underground bunkers below Bab al-Aziziya and surrounded himself with a small circle of power and patronage centred on his family. He called himself 'Brother Leader', but 'I am Libya' is what he told his women and he meant it. Many young Libyans began to realise that he had stolen their country and replaced it with a parody. The world changed around him and he lacked the intellect to adjust to it.

Often overlooked is the way Libya's oil wealth was spent. From the Libyan point of view, it loomed large and still does. It is at least as important as the military reforms. Benghazi was a city the modern world had nearly destroyed and then left behind. It was a place where the people who had long been marginalized by a succession of colonial powers were now last in the queue for the oil money controlled by Muammar Ghaddafi.

Tribes still mattered in East Libya. Out in the hinterland and in the smaller cities the great tribes had been pursuing a life which had changed little since the eleventh century. Some argue persuasively that my emphasis on the tribes stems from a colonial mindset; they make a fair point, and what follows needs reading with that in mind. The Sa'adi tribes of Cyrenaica were the true heirs of the Hilalian migration who occupied their land by right of conquest. They were, in this regard, noblemen or Hurr by birth. They had supported King Idris and were rewarded with places at his high table. Below them in the social order were the Marabtin, or client tribes, who were not true Arabs. As Ghaddafi's regime adapted to the realities of government it turned away from the Sa'adi tribes to the Ghaddadfa tribe of Arab–Berber origin and its allies in the Sirtica for its trusted lieutenants. Thus, the Sa'adi tribes were now below the salt.

Ghaddafi had made sure that oil wealth flowed through a very few key financial bodies over which he had unprecedented control. He rewarded those who sat at his high table with access to it and those below the salt had to wait upon them for some of it – a sure route to rampant corruption. Thus, the perception grew in East Libya that the wealth generated by its own oil was being siphoned off by Tripoli and, worse still, by tribes which had usurped their rightful place. How did this work? Mostly through the Oil and Gas Council and the Libya Investment Authority, one of the world's largest sovereign wealth funds and the holding company which managed Ghaddafi's wealth.

The personality cult of Ghaddafi had made him enemies. Dr Mohamed Yusuf Al-Magariaf was one. Sometime Libyan ambassador to India, he formed the National Front for the Salvation of Libya (NFSL) on 7 October 1981 at a press conference in Khartoum. The group was allowed to operate in the Sudan until President Jaafar Nimeiry fell from power in a coup in 1985. It conducted a campaign to end the Ghaddafi regime with the aid of a shortwave radio station and a newsletter called Al-*Inqadh* – translated roughly as 'Salvation'.

In the 1980s – and well into the 1990s – Ghaddafi's regime defeated major plots by the NFSL. In 1984, NFSL members attacked the colonel's residence in Tripoli's Bab al-Aziziya military compound.

Ghaddafi's enemies were a diverse group, but even those in exile were not beyond the reach of his assassins. He focused much of his personal attention on defectors living in exile in the United States, Britain, Egypt, Morocco and the Sudan who, as well as the NFSL, had formed opposition movements such as the Libyan

1. Field Marshal Khalifa Haftar receives the German Foreign Minister, Heiko Maas, at his headquarters in Benghazi on 16 January 2020. Haftar's self-discipline is clearly evident. (DPA Picture Alliance/Alamy Stock Photo)

2. Field Marshall Khalifa Haftar at a security conference in Benghazi in October 2017. He is among the most experienced military leaders in the world today. (Sylvia Buchholz/ Alamy Stock Photo)

3. Egyptian President Sisi rides with military leaders from the Middle East at the opening of the large base at Mursa Matruh in Egypt's Western Desert in July 2017. Honoured among the VIPs is Field Marshal Khalifa Haftar. (Zuma Press Inc/Alamy Stock Photo)

4. Colonel Muammar Ghaddafi, forceful and charismatic leader of the putsch which removed Libya's monarchy in 1969. (MARKA/Alamy Stock Photo)

5. Muammar Ghaddafi in 2011 at the end of his forty-two-year reign in Libya, by now a sad caricature corrupted by absolute power. (Reuters/photograph by Zohra Benserma/ Alamy Stock Photograph)

6. Women protesting on the streets of Benghazi in February 2011. Their relatives had been massacred in Tripoli's notorious Abu Salim Jail. Their protest ignited the revolution against Ghaddafi. (Reuters/photograph by Esam Omram al Fitori/Alamy Stock Photo)

7. General Abdul Fatah Younis al-Obeidi, the flamboyant commander of the Libyan rebel army, in 2011. The contrast in leadership styles between him and Khalifa Haftar is illustrated in this image. He was murdered in June 2011. (Reuters/photograph by Mohamed Salem/Alamy Stock Photo)

8. Military improvisation is shown by the modifications to this pick-up deployed by the rebels in the dunes near Misrata against Ghaddafi's forces in February 2011. (Reuters/Alamy Stock Photo)

9. The oil refinery at Ras Lanuf, one of the oil facilities in Libya's oil crescent under attack in 2011. (Reuters/Alamy Stock Photo)

10. Urban warfare in Benghazi in 2017. It is hard for an invading army to remove fanatical defenders from the cement rubble of demolished buildings. (Reuters/photograph by Esam Omram al Fatori/Alamy Stock Photograph)

11. Desert warfare. An exposed and vulnerable rebel fighter aiming an anti-tank weapon in the desert hinterland around the Gulf of Sirte. Fighters and supply columns in the desert are easy pickings for drones. (Paul Conroy/Alamy Stock Photo)

12. Abandoned Libyan tanks in the desert near Ouadi Doum, Ghaddafi's base in Northern Chad, following the defeat in March 1987 of Ghaddafi's forces at Chadian hands. (SFM Titti Soldati/Alamy Stock Photographs)

13. Benghazi's port was bombed during the Second World War. Sunken ships were cleared by the British to allow food imports when the Italian farmers fled the British 8th Army in 1942. (Trinity Mirror/Mirrorpix/Alamy Stock Photo)

14. Idris al-Senussi, hereditary leader of the Islamic Senussi sect, sometime Emir of Cyrenaica and King of Libya from 1951 to 1969. (History and Art Collection/Alamy Stock Photo)

15. A bellicose Benito Mussolini struts his stuff in Italian Libya in the 1930s. His fascist regime triggered unprecedented brutality in East Libya. (Barry Iverson Collection/Alamy Stock Photo)

16. Tripoli's Red Castle, the seat of Ottoman power in Libya between 1551 and 1912. (Giuseppe Masci/Alamy Stock Photo)

base and assessing the loyalty of his senior officers. They needed the cooperation of the NTC and it was becoming likely that some of its members were unreliable. It was at this point that NATO reassessed the role of the NTC and forced its leader, Mahmood Jibril, to change his cabinet. The failure to bring the killers to justice seriously undermined public confidence in the NTC as a future government of Libya, and in the judiciary. It angered the Obeidat tribe, which still awaits and continues to press for justice. The NTC was divided and weakened.

As Ghaddafi's grip on East Libya faltered, Islamist jihadists began to emerge. Ghaddafi's propaganda machine had asserted in February 2011 that an 'Islamic Emirate of Derna' had been declared under the leadership of one Abdul-Hakim al-Hasadi, who was said to be a Guantanamo returnee. Al-Hasadi denied having been incarcerated in Guantanamo and stated that there was no Islamic Emirate. This led some observers to assume that Ghaddafi's propagandists had raised the spectre of an al-Qaeda linkage with Derna in order to legitimise his military response to the uprising in the eastern cities. However, a captured al-Qaeda list of foreign fighters in Iraq contained the names of more jihadists from Derna than any other city. That, and the subsequent history of Islamist activity in Derna, led some of us to revise this view. Events such as the killing of Abdul Fatah Younis may explain why. Seeds of religious intolerance germinated in the Arab Spring. Have their shoots borne fruit and multiplied?

So far, the story has been told from an East Libyan perspective. Here tribes matter and Ghaddafi had snubbed them and, they believed, used the oil beneath their homelands to favour his own tribe and its allies and to pursue his own erratic ambitions. West Libya, the old province of Tripolitania, was different. Ghaddafi had lost the east, but he began to lose his war when two major cities in the west turned against him. They were Misrata to his east and Zintan in the Western Mountains with access to his south. What is more, the military expenditure of the NATO countries increased rapidly. The military hardware and software of the early twenty-first century was lavishly deployed on behalf of the NTC. Battle management aircraft, such as AWACS and surveillance drones, were brought into play as were missiles with pinpoint accuracy. The UK was preparing to use Apache attack helicopters operating from HMS *Ocean*, an amphibious assault ship.

Misrata Rebels

The case of Misrata illustrates the characteristics of the Libyan civil war. It has it all, from the first protests to the evolution of street fighters into organised fighting units, the ejection of Ghaddafi's army and the aftermath, including the resort by some to violent retribution.[12]

Misrata, on the Mediterranean coast some 187 kilometres west of Tripoli and 825 kilometres east of Benghazi, is Libya's third-largest city, with 55,000 inhabitants. It is self-contained and self-reliant, and fierce independence, a mercantile and martial spirit and civic cohesion have long been among its characteristics. On 17 February a small street protest began in sympathy with the people of Benghazi. The police arrested some of the protesters, so more people joined. Then the police opened fire and around seventy protesters were shot, causing the growing crowd to react angrily, heaving rocks and Molotov cocktails at the hastily withdrawing police. An angry hunt ensued for Ghaddafi's henchmen and they fled the city. Two weeks later Ghaddafi responded, launching tanks and armoured vehicles at the rebels, who fended them off with improvised anti-tank defences such as

---

12. Small Arms Revue, http://www.smallarmssurvey.org/ fileadmin/docs/H-Research_Notes/SAS-Research-Note-18.pdf, and Libyastories.com.

sand-filled shipping containers. They were ingenious in devising methods of attacking the tanks: they lay down blankets soaked in diesel, which became caught in the tank tracks, and then threw Molotov cocktails from a side street to set the blankets alight. Despite their inventiveness and courage, however, the city was badly damaged and the casualties amounted to around 1,000 dead, some of whom were shot by Ghaddafi's snipers posted in abandoned buildings.

It was a slow and deadly fightback and characterised by all the hallmarks of urban warfare. There was no central leadership in the early stages, but local leaders began to emerge and adopt *noms de guerre*. The loyalty to leaders is a prominent characteristic of these fighting groups and is intensified by tribal, religious and clan relationships.

Gradually, various street fighting groups acquired weapons and leadership and gelled into revolutionary brigades. In Misrata some of the leadership was supplied by Islamists long suppressed by Ghaddafi. A similar pattern emerged in the other centres where fighting was at its most intense, namely Zintan and Benghazi. The fighting brigades managed to gain control over the large quantities of arms which Ghaddafi had accumulated over the years. These included an especially large number of tanks which they learned to operate effectively. They rapidly learned to operate the hi-tech Global Positioning Systems and Google Earth and fight in large and coordinated battle groups. But despite the improvements they made, the accusation that they were disorganised, ill disciplined and reckless has stuck.

The problem was fragmentation. How to coordinate these tightly knit, introspective revolutionary brigades was not only a tactical challenge but a political problem. Urban warfare is relatively new in the history of warfare. It is easier to defend than to attack in the three-dimensional cityscape, especially in heavily damaged, concrete-rich ruins. Adapting the revolutionary brigades to open warfare was also challenging. In Misrata the problem was partially solved by the formation of the Misratan Union of Revolutionaries. By November 2011, 236 revolutionary brigades had joined and a rough head count suggests that there were some 40,000 individual members. A small number of brigades refused to join the Union of Revolutionaries and were thus unregulated. Estimates vary but it was probably nine – a seemingly insignificant number, but enough to cause problems once the siege of Misrata was over and Ghaddafi's forces had withdrawn. Even today, these unregulated brigades remain the main obstacle to peace in the country and are responsible for the majority of human rights violations. Serious allegations include one in January 2012, when Médecins Sans Frontières stopped its work in detention centres in Misrata because its medical staff were being asked to patch up detainees midway through torture sessions so they could go back for more abuse.

In August 2011, Misratans broke out of the brutal siege of their city by Colonel Ghaddafi's forces and attacked their neighbours in Tawergha. Ghaddafi had once lavished money and favour on Tawergha and now, accused of crimes against Misratan civilians during the siege, all 35,000 or so residents fled and the town was systematically looted and destroyed by vengeful Misratans. Ghaddafi's forces had laagered in Tawergha while conducting the siege of Misrata and some of the young men of the town joined them in the fighting. Accusations of rape have been levied at them, though not yet substantiated.

The classification of Libyan armed groups during and after the revolution of 17 February is often misused. The word *thuwwar* is used often to describe the groups formed and fought during the battle against Ghaddafi. It has no military classification because it translates roughly into English as 'freedom fighters'. After Ghaddafi was killed there was a breakdown in civil society and law and order – a security vacuum – and a number of militia units were formed to fill the security gap. A number of criminal groups posed as *thuwwars*, and still do, and extremist groups with Salfaist/Wahabi/Jihadist links have also grown in importance in the post-Ghaddafi security vacuum. They are prominent in Benghazi and Derna but, while they may derive support from external sources, they have little popular support. It is important – but not easy, as they proliferated wildly – to distinguish between these and the true *thuwwars*.

Much the same process of evolution of anti-Ghaddafi *thuwwars* took place in the city of Zintan and neighbourhood towns in the Western Mountains: the Zintan Revolutionaries' Military Council was formed in May 2011 to organise the military efforts and effectiveness of twenty-three militias in this region. This is an area in which numerous Berbers live and they had been badly treated by Ghaddafi. The region reaches westward to the Tunisian border and the Zintani *thuwwars* threatened the southern approaches to Tripoli via Gharian.

The Arabic word *liwa* denotes a force of around 10,000 fighters and is made up of *kata'ib*. The singular of this is *katiba* and is used by a number of sources as a general term for armed groups. It is translated into English as 'brigade' and in Arab military parlance is a force of anything between several hundred and a thousand fighters. In the Libyan context the word is used for units of battalion size. The word *katiba* is appropriate to units formed in Misrata, Zintan and Benghazi because these cities were the recipients of NATO arms deliveries and coordination with NATO's belligerent no-fly zone. A *katiba* was usually split into smaller units of up to 200 fighters. These were called by the accepted Arab word *sariyya* or, in the British Army, a company. The word militia is used often by me and others as a general term. It means exactly what most of us understand: a body of citizen soldiers as opposed to professional soldiers.

Taking Tripoli

With Misrata and Zintan turned against Ghaddafi, the next step was to take Tripoli. Preparation for Dawn Mermaid, as the operation was codenamed, began in April 2011 and was agreed with President Sarkozy. A rebel spy in Tripoli who was well placed to do so began to accumulate information about Ghaddafi's security, intelligence and military apparatus and to seek out rebel sympathisers in key roles. He managed to locate seventy-two military officers who were ready to help the rebels. They included al-Barani Ashkal, commander-in-chief of the guard at Ghaddafi's military compound at Bab al-Aziziya.

Military operation rooms, safehouses, barracks, police stations, radars and telephone centres were located and mapped. In all, eighty-two sites were identified for NATO to target from the air. Trained and armed infiltrators were inserted into Tripoli by sea, equipped to communicate with rebel planners and able to purchase arms in Tripoli.

British special forces had carried out a dangerous and testing assignment. They had infiltrated the city and placed hi-tech transmitters on key targets to mark them for attack by NATO aircraft. They managed to highlight thirty-four of the most critical in this way and thereby saved collateral damage and unnecessary loss of civilian lives. One valuable windfall for the rebels came when they broke into the government communications system and harvested calls between top leaders including Ghaddafi's sons. The rebels broadcast some of them to make the leadership aware that their communications had been compromised.

Early in May, NATO, Qatari and UAE trainers entered Zintan and began training elite rebel forces from East Libya in the Western Mountains. It is the role of the Qataris that is of special interest. They sent not only trainers but special advisers, special forces and military equipment and, unlike NATO, channelled their financial and material aid to favoured groups, especially the

Tripoli Military Council that had set up in the mountains to train and arm for the assault on Tripoli. They chose the Libyan Islamic Fighting Group for special attention.

The French began to smuggle arms into Tripoli and brief rebel cells about their tasks when the expected invasion by Misratan and Zintani forces invaded the city. But the assassination of General Younis on 28 July put the wind up the planners. They were now insecure about the stability of the National Transition Council and decided to push the plan forward in case the anti-Ghaddafi forces fell apart in disarray. As we have seen, NATO forced a change of the NTC cabinet but the sense of unease persisted. It was around this time that Turkey declared her support for the rebels.

On 13 August the western city of Zawiyah fell to a home-grown rebellion and the key southern city of Gharian, on the route to Tripoli from the south, capitulated to the rebels. This meant that Tripoli was now isolated by a ring of rebel-held cities and Ghaddafi's forces began to crumble. His mercenaries began to desert him. The rebel forces of Misrata, Zintan and Zawiyah were preparing to descend on Tripoli and take the city when given the go-ahead by the NTC.

NATO became impatient and signalled its desire to bring the ground attack forward. On 19 August, just after the Ramadan fast was over for the day, NTC Chairman Mustafa Abdel Jalil broadcast a speech that was the signal for the Tripoli rebel cells to emerge and go about their planned tasks of attacking installations and command posts, securing neighbourhoods and setting up roadblocks.

Rebel forces from Zintan, supported by precision strikes from NATO air forces and Apache ground attack helicopters, pushed forwards towards Tripoli via Gharian in the south, Misrata in the east and Zuwara in the west. The advance units were quickly at the gates of Tripoli.

Ghaddafi, who had broadcast on TV interminably, deludedly and belligerently, was now deserted by the generals he had put in charge of Tripoli's defence. They simply downed arms and left town. It was the final blow.

The city fell to the rebels. One small battle – that around Ghaddafi's Bab al-Aziziya – was recorded by Qatari media and made one man, Abdelhakim Belhaj, into a hero. When the dust settled there were those who saw this as a deliberate attempt to hijack the glory.

On 28 August, after eight months of intense conflict, Ghaddafi was on the run. He ran for Sirte, in his tribal homeland, to make a last stand. His son Mutassim was already there because it was his forward HQ from where he commanded Ghaddafi's forces on the eastern front. Khamis Ghaddafi, who commanded the 32nd (Khamis) Brigade, was killed on 29 August by a NATO missile which destroyed his convoy. Niger was the destination of Ghaddafi's playboy son Saadi. He is said to have escaped there with the assistance of a colourful and loquacious bodyguard from New Zealand who claims to have been trained by the Australian army. Saif al-Islam made his way to Bani Walid, the stronghold of the Warfella tribe that was still mostly loyal to his father. He was captured on 19 November by a Zintani militia operating in the south near the Libyan border. They took him back to Zintan where he was imprisoned as a hostage of advantage.

Sirte was then besieged by *thuwwars* from Misrata, Benghazi and Zintan who bombarded it with Grad missiles and heavy artillery. Ghaddafi and his close circle are believed to have sheltered in damaged houses and moved around to escape the relentless bombardment.

In beleaguered Sirte, on 20 October, Mutassim Ghaddafi organised and led a column of around fifty heavily armed troop carriers to take Muammar Ghaddafi, his remaining loyalists and a few civilians to safety. He may have hoped he could fight his column past the besieging *thuwwars* and make it to Niger. But on its way out of town the column was hit by a NATO air strike, which suggests that it was detected easily. One armoured vehicle was destroyed. The column was later struck by cluster bombs from a NATO aircraft, killing many. A Misratan *thuwwar* located them and engaged with some of the survivors. Muammar Ghaddafi and others attempted to escape across some cultivated country and fetched up near drainage ditches under a road. Misratan fighters caught up with them and one of Ghaddafi's bodyguards threw a grenade which bounced back and exploded, wounding Ghaddafi himself and killing some of his guard.

The fighters found Ghaddafi and began to beat him up. Some say he was sodomised with a bayonet. By the time he reached hospital his body was lifeless. One story claims that he was shot using the gold-plated pistol of which he had been so proud. The Misratans also caught Mutassim Ghaddafi who was, apparently, walking wounded. He was taken to a hotel where he was seen smoking and drinking water, but by the end of the day he appears to have suffered a fatal wound and died.

Vengeful Carnage or Just Revenge?

The siege of Misrata had been savage. Ghaddafi's forces are said to have used rape as a weapon and some of the Misratan *thuwwars* had revenged themselves on the black tribe of Tawergha as we have seen. There was certainly a disturbing descent into cruelty as the civil war neared its end. It was one of a cluster of characteristics which came together to distinguish the Libyan experience of the Arab Spring from others, and it must trouble the governments that rushed to the aid of the rebels in February 2011. Human Rights Watch has suggested:

Anti Ghaddafi forces captured 150 persons after the battle [of Sirte]. They transported some 70 of these persons to Misrata and held them in custody, but at least 53 and possibly 66 people were found dead the next day at the nearby Mahari Hotel.

Ghaddafi employed mercenaries from the Sahel and the Saharan Tuareg. Prior to the Libyan uprising, the country hosted approximately one million African workers, many of whom were employed in construction, garbage collection, domestic work and other low-wage jobs. A number of workers from Niger were imprisoned by Libyan militias who believed them to have been Ghaddafi's mercenaries. The treatment of some of them is reported to be brutal and the International Organisation for Migration worked to get them released. Until the Libyan government was able to assert control over the many armed militias the treatment of these prisoners, and others from Chad and Mali, would continue to cause unease. But the NTC was unable to disband or integrate militias with the army.

Joe Stork, deputy Middle East and North Africa director of Human Rights Watch, stated on 5 February 2013:

> The [Libyan] government acknowledges that about 8,000 people are being detained across Libya, but only about 5,600 of these are in facilities controlled to some degree by the military or the Interior and Justice ministries.

The independence of the *thuwwars* meant that they were not regulated by the NTC. They did not disband after Ghaddafi's death. Their detention of prisoners was therefore unregulated and often brutal.

The Tuareg had also supplied Ghaddafi with mercenaries whom he armed lavishly with modern weapons. When his regime fell his Tuareg units fled back to Mali with their considerable weaponry and military training. The iron law of unforeseen consequences now made itself felt.

The National Transition Council Fails to Control the Militias

The virtual destruction of the standing army, police force and intelligence services left a power vacuum which was temporarily filled by armed militias. They cohered to form power-broking groups and this was, and is, probably the greatest challenge to the will of the Libyan people as expressed in recent elections. Per Libyastories.com:

> On 5 October 2011, a military commander from Misrata, Salem Juha, was appointed Defence Minister by the Libyan Interim National Council. However, reports coming from Tripoli in the last few days suggest that he has a difficult job on his hands, despite the suggestion that he is acceptable to the Islamists among the many Libyan militia commanders. Abdelhakim Belhaj, who heads the Tripoli Military Council, is warning of potential conflict among armed groups which have stayed in Tripoli. Belhaj, a sometime member of the Libyan Islamist Fighting Group which Ghaddafi suppressed in the 1990s, is widely quoted as saying, 'We need to end the presence of heavy weapons and keep them from proliferating, except among authorized parties' – by which he means his own Tripoli Military Council. He may have a problem.
>
> At a news conference in Tripoli a militia commander, Abdullah Ahmed Naker, claimed to have 22,000 armed men at his disposal as he announced the formation of a Tripoli Revolutionist Council. He asserted that his forces are already in control of 75 per cent of the capital and that Belhaj could only call on 2,000 armed supporters. Clearly Salem Juha, and the Interim National Council, needs to assert control in Tripoli.

The Siege of Bani Walid

There was one more siege to go and its story tells us something significant. A year after Ghaddafi's death, in October 2012, Omran Shaban, the Misratan militiaman who found Ghaddafi hiding from a NATO air strike in a storm drainage pipe in Sirte, was captured and killed in Bani Walid, the last foothold of Ghaddafi loyalists. Bani Walid is the desert stronghold of the Warfella tribe and had capitulated to anti-Ghaddafi forces on 17 October 2011. Since that time, the Bani Walid leadership had been at odds with the Misratans, who believed that Ghaddafists had been given shelter in the town. The death of Omran Shaban was a flash point, launching the Misratan militias on Bani Walid and resulting in twenty-two deaths and 200 non-fatal casualties. The refugee problem the siege caused was acute: on 22 October 2012 the International Committee of the Red Cross estimated that 25,000 people had fled the urban area.

What does this tell us about Libya after the death of Ghaddafi? It makes it clear that Misrata was able and willing to act independently of central government. It also makes it clear that the militias were not disbanded a year after Ghaddafi's death. They were the tail wagging the Libyan dog.

Libya's Future in the Balance

There were two non-NATO countries involved in the fight against Ghaddafi and their investment was heavy. They were the United Arab Emirates and Qatar. Their involvement reflects the rivalry which emerged in Libya with the taking of Tripoli and still troubles the Arab world.

Let us look at the prize. Libya is strategically important and has vast oil reserves below its desert hinterland. In its recent history it was seen as the northern gateway into Africa for European trade and today, were it peaceful, it could offer lucrative transit and trading facilities. As things stood on the death of Ghaddafi, the main trade between sub-Saharan Africa and Libya's 2,000-kilometre coastline was in people. But the people traffickers would not survive the competition offered by a stable Libya investing in proper trade routes and establishing financial institutions to facilitate trade. There were other positive outcomes to a stable Libya, for example the Great Man-made River, a network of water delivery pipelines which could be tapped into the desiccated Sahel regions now suffering from the effects of climate change. These attractive advantages were not pursued by Ghaddafi, who was too narrow minded to visualise and implement them. But they could be exploited now.

As well as altruistic motivations, the advantages of an alliance with a stable Libya would not be far from the minds of the rulers of the United Arab Emirates and Qatar. They may have been what attracted Turkey's support for the NTC. Nor would the rivalry with a stable Libya for influence in Africa have slipped their attention. Qatar was and still is at odds with the UAE and Saudi Arabia, and this not only complicated the war to oust Ghaddafi but set the rivalry alight at the moment of his fall.

On Qatar's part, the Qatari emir, Sheik Abdul Hamed bin Khalifa al-Thani, had a strong family connection with Libya. His is a very small country with huge natural gas fields at its disposal. It is thus very rich and pursues an active foreign policy. It is well equipped to wage propaganda war and did so on behalf of Libya's NTC by means of its al-Jazeera media empire. It set up a TV station for the NTC called Libya al-Ahrar, and favoured Abdelhakim Belhaj in its coverage of the battle for Aziziya. It was Libya al-Ahrar which intercepted incriminating phone calls between Ghaddafi's family members and broadcast them in the lead-up to the taking of Tripoli. Qatar also supplied the NTC with an estimated 20,000 tons of weapons in eighteen shipments. But its most significant contribution came when its special forces fought alongside the Libyan *thuwwars*, giving expert advice to their commanders and, in effect, providing the planning and staff work that gave the rebels a priceless advantage.

It is difficult to see NATO's involvement in the Libyan civil war without coming to the conclusion that it was entered into without understanding the special nature of Libya or the effects the fall of Ghaddafi would have on Libya's neighbours. In contrast, it is likely that the involvement of Qatar and the UAE was driven by long-term aims. As Khalifa Haftar prepares his campaign to cleanse Libya, as he would say, how will the foreign intervention in the Libyan uprising play out?

6

DEMOCRACY OR THEOCRACY?

Haftar's New World – Early Signs and Portents

Khalifa Haftar and what remained of the young officers who had plotted the overthrow of King Idris and the expulsion of the British and American military from Libya would not, surely, have hoped for the civil war that had just convulsed their country, left so many dead, displaced so many from their accustomed homes and created a security vacuum which placed them in constant danger. What was Haftar's world like a year after the Benghazi street protests set the country alight?

The British, French and US, fearful of repeating the mistakes made after the fall of Saddam Hussein in Iraq, had withdrawn their considerable military might and left Libya in the hands of the National Transitional Council. They must have known that the NTC had limited tenure and was weak. Power, as leading authority on Libya Jason Pack argues, had leaked from the centre to the periphery. The events in Misrata support Dr Pack's hypothesis. The onlookers should have predicted that the apparatus used in the ruthless exercise of power by Muammar Ghaddafi would be decapitated and collapse. If they did, they took precious little care to ensure that the power vacuum they had helped to create was filled, even temporarily.

So, by 17 February 2012, when Libyans should have been celebrating the first anniversary of the Benghazi uprising which triggered the fall of Ghaddafi, their new leaders had still failed to control the numerous revolutionary militias known as *thuwwars* that had formed during the civil war. The militiamen themselves argued that they fought to topple Ghaddafi and were entitled to say who ran their country. And since they were heavily armed, some with artillery and tanks, they easily asserted their authority because the regular army was weakened and there was no real police force. What was more, the Ghaddafi regime had destroyed civic society and outlawed political parties. Indeed, at the height of Muammar Ghaddafi's power Libya was a near equal to some of the heavily regulated societies such as North Korea in terms of the proportion of its people involved in its security and control apparatus.

The management and control of the extensive state security and intelligence network had been concentrated in Ghaddafi's hands and those of his blood relatives, relatives of his second wife Safia Farkash, and members of his own tribe and its allies. In fact, it is not unreasonable to state that Ghaddafi and his regime remained in power for so long because he had unlimited personal control of the intelligence gathering and of a very large system of informants and enforcers pervading every aspect of civilian and military life.

But all this collapsed after his death. Ordinary Libyans lacked the democratic machinery to fill the power vacuum, so what may be called post-revolutionary militias appeared. Few were formed for altruistic reasons. Many were formed by military entrepreneurs who spotted the opportunities available for promoting their own causes or their personal wealth. The greater majority of these warring militias were on the government payroll and it is very likely that payment was made by the government to the militia commanders, some of whom had become very rich by inflating their nominal rolls and pocketing the pay for phantom militiamen.

In this regard an open letter to the Libyan House of Representatives from the Lawyers for Justice in Libya stated, 'Mounting evidence suggests that many of the groups responsible for such grave human rights violations are largely supported and funded through criminal activities. Human, drugs and arms smuggling, has allowed many to profit illegally and immorally from the on-going crisis. These criminal activities have prolonged the disruption of peace in the country.'

The capital, Tripoli, was a case in point. There were at least seven armed militias controlling the city, one of which was led by the sometime Islamist fighter Abdelhakim Belhaj. He now headed the new entity called the Tripoli Military Council. As we have seen, however, rival Abdullah Ahmed Naker claimed to have 22,000 armed men at his disposal and control of 75 per cent of the capital.

More significantly, *thuwwars* from other regions of Libya controlled parts of the capital. One of them was from Misrata and had been in a gunfight with Belhaj's militia. A further *thuwwar* from the town of Zintan controlled Tripoli's international airport. This Zintan militia had captured Ghaddafi's favourite son, Saif al-Islam, and had him incarcerated in Zintan, apparently without access to a lawyer. The Berbers from the Western Mountains also maintained a militia in Tripoli. Clearly, they intend to see that the Berbers, long suppressed by Ghaddafi, were not marginalised in the new Libya. The new Libyan government seemed to have abandoned Misrata to its militias, of which there were thought to be 170 or so. Some of the militias were accused of mistreating suspected Ghaddafi loyalists. According to the UN Commission for Human Rights, there had been torture, extrajudicial executions and rape of both men and women.

Militant Islamists Show Their Hand

The militant Islamists were so proud of their act of vandalism that they broadcast their mobile phone images around the world. They desecrated the graves of the British and Commonwealth Second World War dead in the Beloun Farm Cemetery in Benghazi and symbolically attacked its monumental cross with a sledgehammer. They broke a number of gravestones, especially those on which the star of David had been carved. This was no spontaneous vandalism – the group was armed, well prepared and clearly felt that it was both right and righteous.

The Commonwealth War Graves Commission had maintained this and other cemeteries in Libya throughout the reign of King Idris and the dictatorship of Ghaddafi. The soldiers buried there had given their lives to free Libya from the often brutal rule of its Italian colonists. The vandals were obviously ignorant of this crucial fact; the British role in freeing their forebears had been written out of Libyan history by Ghaddafi.

The transitional government in Libya was embarrassed by the distressing images, not least because British serviceman had once again risked their lives, this time to release ordinary Libyans from Ghaddafi's oppressive regime. I knew Beloun Farm Cemetery well as it was close to our family home. Its desecration was an early sign that militant Islamists were active in Benghazi and were confident of immunity from the law. No one was apprehended or charged.

One estimate (probably an educated guess) was that there were around 2,000 militant Islamists in Libya. That is not many. It was, however, a significant number, because they were ruthless, and they practised the process of entryism, hijacking groups of well-meaning local activists to promote their cause.

Democracy Threatened

On Wednesday 8 August 2012, Libya's new democratically elected congress began to assume power. It elected Mohammed Youssef

Magariaf as its President. Magariaf won 113 votes from the 200-strong congress against the independent candidate Ali Zidan, who gained eighty-five votes.

President Magariaf was the leader of the National Front Party – known as the National Front for the Salvation of Libya during the Ghaddafi era. It was Magariaf who had recruited Khalifa Haftar in Chad to establish the military arm of his National Front for the Salvation of Libya, from which he resigned while in USA. He was, we will recall, an economist and former Libyan ambassador to India who was born in Benghazi in 1940. His election is seen as an important boon for Benghazi, where many feared they were being side-lined.

President Magariaf now had less than thirty days to select a prime minister, begin the process of drafting a new constitution and start organising parliamentary elections. He selected Dr Mustafa Abushagur, a long-time exile from Ghaddafi's Libya for prime minister. Among the numerous problems about which Magariaf and Abushagur were distressed to hear almost immediately after they took their posts was that unidentified gunmen in Benghazi had shot dead a Libyan Army general and high-ranking defence ministry official, Mohamed Hadia al-Feitouri. Al-Feitouri was one of Ghaddafi's army generals who defected early to the 17 February movement. He was one of a number of ex-Ghaddafi men who had been assassinated in Benghazi by unknown killers.

Ghaddafi had not liked Benghazi much. The city had been ruled for some time by his henchwoman Huda Ben Amer, who had first come to his attention as he sat in his Tripoli bunker watching a TV relay of a public hanging in Benghazi. The victim was slow to die and thrashed about on the end of the rope, and Ben Amer had hurried his demise by hanging onto his legs. Ghaddafi was impressed and appointed her mayor of Benghazi, where she became known as Huda the Executioner. She fled to Tripoli soon after the February uprising and her villa in Benghazi was razed to the ground.

This helps to explain, but does not excuse, the killing of fourteen more high-ranking officers who had served in Ghaddafi's military but changed sides and were deployed to Benghazi by the new transitional government. No one was arrested for these assassinations. The view that the Libyan military should purge itself of the remnants of Ghaddafi's regime was not without adherents in Benghazi.

The most pressing of the many problems facing Libya's new government was the large number of anti-Ghaddafi militias still bearing arms. They had been particularly active in Benghazi, which was badly hit by violence. Among the targets of attack were the United Nations, the Red Cross, a convoy carrying the British Ambassador, and the Tunisian consulate. The lack of regard for normal diplomatic freedoms pointed to a growing disaster.

Then, global attention was focused on Benghazi on 11 September 2012, when the US consulate was stormed by armed militiamen. US Ambassador Christopher Stevens died of smoke inhalation while trapped inside the consulate, and three other Americans were killed in the attack or the rescue attempt that followed. In response, US drones began conducting reconnaissance missions over Benghazi, and a counter-terrorist unit was readied to go to Libya. Two American warships, Arleigh Burke-class destroyers USS *Laboon* and USS *McFaul*, were also deployed off the Libyan coast. There were a number of CIA operatives in the city probably trying to locate and purchase the MANPADS (man portable air defence systems) which had been looted from Ghaddafi's extensive weapon stores. They were spirited out of town fast. FBI agents were waiting to go to Benghazi to find out who killed Ambassador Stevens but appeared to be stuck in Tripoli. In the end, no retributive action was taken by the US. Was that a mistake?

There are more questions about this unusual event. Was Ambassador Stevens overconfident? Was his protection in Benghazi good enough? Had the CIA read the situation in Benghazi badly?

There was no US Consul in Benghazi and Ambassador Stevens appears to have covered the duties himself, mostly from his embassy in Tripoli. The consulate was housed in a rented villa and guarded by a five-man security team from the US diplomatic protection service and a rota of Libyan guards employed by a small British security company called Blue Mountain. This company had a Libyan partner and other security contracts in Benghazi. The Blue Mountain guards were armed with Tasers and were thus not employed or equipped to defend the consulate against a heavily armed attack. Their British manager had left Benghazi following a difference of views with the company's Libyan partner. Two of his sometime employees had earlier blown a substantial hole in the consulate's perimeter wall with an IED in revenge for their dismissal.

The US consulate in Benghazi was the last to fly a foreign flag. The British had evacuated their diplomatic personnel from their Benghazi consulate after an attempt on their ambassador's life in broad daylight in a well-guarded part of the city. This incident must surely have focused the attention of Secretary of State Hilary Clinton's Libya watchers in Washington. The British had been useful allies of the US, with whom they had exchanged intelligence in the past, and they had long and well-earned experience of diplomacy in Benghazi. The Red Cross had also left the city after its premises were attacked. They are usually the last to leave in such circumstances.

The Ansar al-Sharia militia brigade was the most likely perpetrator of the well-organised attack, and Ambassador Stevens' death seems to have been a deplorable but secondary outcome. But there are said to have been connections between Ansar al-Sharia and al-Qaeda in the Islamic Maghreb, and its rhetoric had certainly been aimed at the US for some time. Wouldn't this have been well known before 11 September 2012?

There were other pointers which should have alerted the US diplomats in Libya to potential dangers. 11 September was the anniversary of the killing by the US in Pakistan of Abou Yahya al-Libi, the al-Qaeda second-in-command. He was a Libyan, and revenge taken in Libya for his killing would have been gruesome publicity for the reach and power of al-Qaeda.

Ansar al-Sharia, the Takfiri-Salafist-jihadist group based mainly in Benghazi and Derna, issued this uncompromising statement in the wake of Ambassador Stevens' death:

> The goal of Ansar al-Sharia brigade is to implement the laws of Allah on the land, and reject the human implemented laws and earthly made constitutions. There will be nothing ruling in this country other than the laws of Allah.

There was some speculation about Ambassador Stevens' diary, in which he is supposed to have expressed his suspicion that he was on an al-Qaeda hit list. Perhaps he was. There certainly was a hit list in Benghazi. It was aimed at killing senior police and military officers who had served in the Ghaddafi regime. But Ambassador Stevens was popular in Benghazi. He had been posted there very soon after the 17 February uprising and helped those who were attempting to form the new government in Libya immeasurably. He had earned the thanks of the people of Benghazi and, tragically, may have felt safe among them. His advisers and superiors in the State Department should have taken more care of him. So, the real question is, was the management of the US consulate in Benghazi effective?

On 12 September, just hours after Ambassador Stevens was killed, the Libyan government dismissed Hussein Abu Humaida, the head of the Security Directorate in Benghazi. On 16 September it appointed the veteran police chief Colonel Salah Al-Din Awad Doghman with the title of Assistant Undersecretary at the Interior Ministry. But the Libyan police in Benghazi refused to serve under Colonel Doghman. He told Reuters, 'When you go to police headquarters, you will find there are no police. The people in charge are not at their desks. They have refused to let me take up my job.' A further sign of a fatal weakness in central government. An Ansar al-Sharia spokesman said that 'if one U.S. soldier arrives, not for the purpose of defending the embassy, but to repeat what happened in Iraq or Afghanistan, be sure that all battalions in Libya and all Libyans will put aside all their differences and rally behind one goal of hitting America and Americans'.

Ruthless, heavily armed gangs can have an effect beyond their numbers and, despite a lack of public support, this may have encouraged Haftar, who by now was engaged in responding to the violence by raising an army. The 'Friday Saving' Facebook page for 21 September carries stories and photographs of some 30,000 Libyans who had marched through Benghazi in an unprecedented protest to demand the disbanding of powerful militias in the wake of the ambassador's killing. Following this, hundreds of demonstrators arrived at the Ansar al-Sharia headquarters on Nasr Square, demanding the brigade leave immediately. Members of Ansar al-Sharia who were acting as guards at Al-Jalaa hospital were also removed by protesters. Around eighty protesters also took control of the headquarters of the Rafallah Al-Sahati brigade, located at a farm in Hawari district, some 15 kilometres from Benghazi's city centre, and the

Ukba bin Nafi'a brigade stronghold was cleared of militiamen. The Libyan police moved in quickly to occupy the bases.

There was more. The Libyan National Army's First Infantry Brigade commander, Colonel Hamid Buheir, confirmed in Benghazi that the Ansar al-Sharia militia had been disbanded but that there were clearly militiamen still at large. A few days later, the colonel was kidnapped by masked men from outside his house. His Salafist kidnappers accused him of being a *kuffer* (unbeliever) and threatened his life but they received a phone call from someone instructing them not to kill him. He was released by being thrown from a car on to a roundabout.

Who made the telephone call? We don't know, but five soldiers from Colonel Buheir's First Infantry Brigade were found dead, shot through the head with their arms tied behind their backs in the Hawiya district of Benghazi.

What do we need to know if we are not versed in Islam? There are Salafists in Libya – and in Egypt and Tunisia – who hold that the principles and practice of early Islam should govern the social and political life of the people. They believe that the true Islam, that of the Prophet Muhammad and the first, second and third generation of his followers, has been obfuscated, contaminated and watered down by constant amendments to its fundamental principles.

Some of the more fervent Salafists abhor the Sufi sects and destroy the tombs of revered holy men, holding that no one person can reinterpret the word of Allah as revealed in Arabic to the Prophet Mohammad and written in the Holy Koran – with the exception of themselves, of course, a strange paradox which is not uncommon among zealots of any creed. The more extreme Salafists – some authorities have called them Salafist jihadists – refuse to become involved in elections because they perceive politics to be anti-Islamic. In their view the will of god supersedes the will of the people. In practice, some members of this faction would impose its interpretation of Sharia law at the point of a gun. For them, to borrow a phrase, the automatic rifle outranks the ballot box. The term *Takfiri* is used by some extremist groups who consider other Muslims or certain groups of Muslims as apostate, for which they prescribe the death penalty and in Libya use this as a justification for killing. The Salafist trend has been vitalized across the Arab world since the Arab Spring and the fall of dictatorships. In one of its militarized manifestations it has emerged as Ansar al-Sharia, which roughly translates as 'Partisans of Sharia Law'. Groups under this name have emerged not just in Libya but in Yemen, Tunisia, Egypt and Morocco. In Libya, however, the group traces its origin to Islamist militias formed to topple Ghaddafi.

Tripoli's Black Friday

Meanwhile, violence escalated in Tripoli. By early August 2013 there was a serious threat of an armed coup. In order to secure the government, it was decided to bring a number of militia brigades to aid the civil powers. It was thus that Colonel Muhamed Musa, commanding the Misratan Brigades of the Libyan Shield Force, entered Tripoli on 11 August to forestall armed attempts to influence the democratic process of the General National Congress. According to the *Libya Herald* dated 11 August 2013:

> More than a thousand vehicles belonging to the Libya Shield forces for Central and Western Regions are reported to have arrived in Tripoli over the past four days. The troops have been deployed to various military locations in and around the capital. The move is to defend it from forces causing instability or planning a move to impose their will on Congress and the government by force.

A report from Cairo carried by *Asharq Al-Awsat* dated
16 November 2013 states:

> At least 40 people have been killed and more than 400 injured
> in the Libyan capital, Tripoli, after militiamen opened fire on
> protesters [in the Gharghur district] calling for their disbandment
> on Friday ... The militia blamed for last week's violence, which
> allegedly included the use of heavy weapons against unarmed
> civilian protesters, are based in the city of Misrata.

Later the casualty figures were revised. It was believed that forty-
seven people were killed and 508 injured, sixty of whom were
sent abroad for treatment. Other casualties received treatment at
private and public medical centres; twenty were in very critical
condition and could not be moved.

In a report from the next day's edition, *Asharq Al-Awsat* stated:

> Residents of the Libyan capital launched a general strike Sunday
> over a militia violence that killed nearly 50 people this weekend.
> The streets of Tripoli were deserted as the vast majority of the city's
> businesses and schools were closed. Bakeries, pharmacies, hospitals
> and gas stations remained open. Sadat Al-Badri, who is head of
> Tripoli's city council, said the strike is to last three days.

There were other disturbing straws in the wind. On 7 August,
Zwai tribesmen stopped oil production in three oilfields lying
beneath their homeland in East Libya in protest against armed
clashes in the south-eastern city of Kufra.

From Car Thief to Small-time War Lord

The oil ports of the Libyan Oil Crescent were also shut down. The
perpetrator was Ibrahim Jadhran, sometime eastern commander
of Petroleum Facilities Guard, who now emerged into the public

domain for a brief but colourful time as a local war lord. He had spent time in Ghaddafi's notorious penal system, from which some never reappeared. The records show he was convicted of car theft but he suggests that the real reason was that he had opposed Muammar Ghaddafi. His brother was mayor of Ajdabiya, where he may have ensured the loyalty of his supporters by putting them on the municipal payroll.

The Jadhran brothers were members of the al-Magharba tribe, as were many of the Petroleum Facilities Guard on the southern shore of the Gulf of Sirte and within the tribe's homeland. Ibrahim Jadhran used his position as commander of the Petroleum Facilities Guard to close down the three oil ports within his command, Ras Lanuf, al-Zuetina, and Sidra. He formed his own company called The Libyan Oil and Gas Corporation and offered crude oil for sale. The brothers were enterprising to say the least. Ibrahim closed the oil ports using the very guards assigned to protect them, the Libyan National Oil Corporation declared *force majeure* and the Tripoli government stated that it would use force to prevent ships from loading oil from the terminals. It was unable to remove Jadhran's Petroleum Facilities Guard.

On Monday 6 January 2014, the Libyan Navy fired on a North Korean-flagged vessel presumed to be on its way to take on crude oil from one of the ports under Jadhran's control. The vessel did not stop. Jadhran then allowed a loaded oil tanker named the *Morning Glory* to set sail from the eastern port of Sidra, but it was promptly stopped and boarded by US Navy Seals.

To compound his defiance to the state, Jadhran became the leader of the short-lived and self-styled Political Bureau of Cyrenaica based in Ajdabiya. He announced a government for Cyrenaica and named Abdraba Abdulhameed al-Barasi, a former Libyan Air Force officer, as prime minister with a cabinet of twenty-four members and threatened to recruit and train a

Cyrenaican Defence Force similar to that which maintained King Idris in power during the 1950s. There was a certain hankering for a return to the gentler days of the past.

On 12 December 2013, the Libyan Embassy in London posted this news:

> Tribal leaders have brokered a deal with the head of the Political Bureau of Cyrenaica, Ibrahim Jadhran, bringing to an end the federalist movement's blockade of three eastern oil terminals.
>
> Elders from the Magharba tribe entered into talks with figures from the federalist movement ten days ago in efforts to bring to a close the deadlock over the oil export terminals. The leader of the Magharba tribe, Saleh Lataiwish, said that its members had responded to calls for the necessary reopening of the terminals. He said that the tribe had held meetings to discuss with 'their sons' an end to actions at Sidra, Ras Lanuf and Zueitina ports. The blockade is set to be lifted this weekend.

It was not lifted. In the end, the Tripoli government bought Mr Jadhran off. It was said to cost a great deal of money, including the back pay of a supposed 20,000 Petroleum Facilities Guardsmen.

An Islamist War Lord Rules Derna

While Jadhran was controlling the oilfields, Derna became the lair of an Islamist warlord called Sufian Ben Qumu. Ben Qumu's 'private' militia had amalgamated with two other radical Islamist armed groups, the Army of the Islamic State of Libya and the Derna branch of Ansar al-Sharia, to form the Shoura Council of Islamic Youth. There were strong elements within this amalgamated group that had ties to al-Qaida, and the Shoura Council of Islamic Youth gained a reputation for violence and militancy. It carried out at least two public executions in Derna which were condemned by Amnesty International. This from the *Libya Herald* dated 20 August 2014:

> The Shura Council of Islamic Youth in Derna has killed an Egyptian man it accused of murder in what is reportedly the second public execution carried out by the group in the town ... [A resident] said the execution took place at a football ground in western Derna. He added that the execution began at around 5 pm, just after Asr prayers.
>
> The execution was the second such public killing in Derna. On 27 July, Islamic Youth put to death two men, one Egyptian and another Libyan, for an alleged murder. This killing received widespread attention after a video of the proceedings was uploaded to the internet. The veracity of the video has been confirmed and shows one man killed by a single gunshot to the head. He is surrounded by around forty members of Islamic Youth, most of whom carry Kalashnikov rifles and wear face masks and military fatigues of one kind or another. One member holds the black flag of al-Qaeda at the centre of proceedings. There are a large number of spectators present in the stands at the football ground but they cannot be seen in the video. The execution is met with the sounds of chanting and applause.

However, there was another very powerful Islamist militia in Derna: the Abu Saleem Martyrs' Brigade, which held the balance of power in the town but maintained turf wars with the Islamic Youth. Here is part of a report carried in the *Libya Herald* on 23 September 2014:

> At least six members of rival Derna Islamist brigades were killed in fighting on Sunday as tensions flared between the town's Abu Saleem Martyrs' Brigade and the Islamic Youth in Derna. The town

today appears to have returned to what has become normality there for more than a year. Over the past twelve months, its radical Islamist brigades have effectively closed the local council, taken control of the court building and liquidated whatever remnants of the town's security forces remained. Four members of Abu Saleem Martyrs' brigade, one Islamic Youth in Derna militiaman along with a civilian perished in the clashes which began on Sunday evening and continued into the early hours of yesterday the morning.

There had been reports of an al-Qaeda training camp in Derna for some time and intelligence from Sebha in Libya's south suggests that there was a constant flow of recruits from the Sahara and Sahel countries. They would pass through on their way to Derna for training and then again on their way back, ready to stiffen al-Qaeda units in their own countries.

The Lawless South

In the south, violence in Kufra between Arab Zawiya tribesmen and the Tebu minority had been going on for some time. Fighting in Kufra first erupted as a smuggling turf war between the well-armed Tebu community and the majority Zawiya tribe. In their attempts to force the government to take decisive action against the Tebu in Kufra the Zawiya also threatened to stop the water supply from the sub-Saharan Aquifer, which was transported in huge cement pipes from near Kufra to the populous coastal cities of Libya. The pipelines and wells are known as the Great Man-made River. The Great Man-made River was begun in 1991 and was said to be the largest engineering undertaking in the world. It was a twenty-five-year project designed to provide half a million cubic metres of water per day to Libya's coastal settlements through a network of pipes totalling over 3,500 kilometres. It was one of the most lauded, and in some ways most worrying, hydrological engineering schemes, which arose out of the search for oil in Libya. It is laudable because it would help to expand agriculture and hence vital food production in the hyper-arid region of the Sahara; it is worrying because the source of the water, the Nubian Sandstone Aquifer System, is considered to be non-renewable and to lie under water-poor regions of Libya, Egypt, Chad and the Sudan.

Abdul Wahab Hassain Qaid, a sometime senior member of the Libyan Islamic Fighting Group, was made commander of border security in the southern part of the country. He is the brother of Abou Yahya al-Libi, Bin Laden's onetime second-in-command, who was killed in Pakistan in June 2012 by an American drone. Quaid was believed to have received 170 million Libyan dinars and a fleet of four-wheel-drive vehicles from Qatar to carry out his duties. This was a provocative appointment by the Tripoli government. The border was of interest to the USA and the al-Qaeda franchises operating in the region. Abdul Wahab Hassain Qaid was now responsible for Libya's volatile south, which borders Algeria, Niger, Chad and the Darfur region of Sudan. Smuggling routes from sub-Saharan Africa to the Mediterranean coast run through the Libyan oasis cities of Murzuq, its neighbouring city Sebha, and Kufra to the east. A massive illicit trade in weapons, petrol and food goods moves south across porous desert borders in return for drugs, alcohol and people moving north.

In Mali, the al-Qaeda franchise Ansar Dine was a threat, and the potential destabilisation of Niger threatened by a restive Tuareg population strengthened by returning Ghaddafi mercenaries was feared. Both these countries have porous borders with Nigeria's impoverished and volatile north in which a further al-Qaeda franchise, Boko Haram, had established a foothold. 'Boko Haram' is the local name for the People Committed to the Propagation of the Prophet's Teachings and Jihad (Jama'atu Ahlis Sunna Lidda'awati Wal-Jihad). It was led by Abubakar

Muhammad Shekau and said to number 3,000 fighters. It is still based in north-eastern Nigeria, conveniently close to the Niger and Mali borders and where people feel ignored by the predominantly Christian government.

Ghaddafi's arms depots had been systematically looted since his downfall, and Libya became a major source of illegal arms exported eastwards into Egypt and Syria, westwards to arm the al-Qaeda franchise fighting in the Chaambi Mountains in Tunisia and southwards into the Sahel countries and Nigeria. Among the major threats to Libya and her neighbours was – and is – the lack of control over the vast amount of weaponry and military hardware which the Ghaddafi regime left in its wake. Because of the fractured nature of the rebellion and the chaotic logistic systems employed by both the Ghaddafi loyalists and the rebel militias, substantial quantities of arms and munitions are unaccounted for to this day.

When it became clear that the NATO and Qatari forces aligned against him had achieved air superiority, Ghaddafi dispersed vast quantities of mines, mortars, artillery, anti-tank and anti-aircraft missiles, tanks and ammunition into abandoned buildings and private properties. These caches were drawn on by both Ghaddafi loyalists and rebel militias during the fluid and chaotic civil war. Few people know how much there was or where it is now. Many are still guessing, including MI6, which England's *Sunday Times* has quoted as its source for the statement that 'there is a million tons of weaponry in Libya – more than the entire arsenal of the British Army – most of it unsecured'.

Following Ghaddafi's demise, much of the weaponry was seized by revolutionary and post-revolutionary militias which were using it to control regions where the rule of law was weak or absent. The mercenary army which Ghaddafi recruited from neighbouring countries to bolster the defence of his regime dispersed homewards after the fall of Tripoli carrying looted weapons and ammunition. In particular, the exodus of his battle-hardened Tuareg warriors, with their considerable armoury, caused instability in Mali and unrest in the other Sahel countries.

The remote and climatically unfavourable southern regions of Libya were declared a military zone and were thus opaque to Libya watchers. This meant that the areas around Ghadames, Ghat, Awbari, Al-Shati, Sebha, Murzuq and Kufra were closed zones of military operations. The long borders between Libya and her southern neighbours – Darfur, Chad and Niger – have always been porous and were now more so. The looted arms may be cached in large quantities in this area and moved out by convoy when the opportunity arises or smuggled in small quantities by what are known as ant smugglers – individuals or small groups who make frequent journeys carrying arms, drugs and migrants.

The near-lawless south of Libya attracted the attention of the al-Qaeda 'emir' Mokhtar Belmokhtar, who may have established a training base there and who was a notorious trafficker in arms, cigarettes and people. Mokhtar Belmokhtar was believed to have mounted the attack in January 2013 on the BP gas facility in southern Algeria from Libya and had been seen in an al-Qaeda video posing with an anti-aircraft rocket launcher which may have been looted from Libya. Chad, Niger and Algeria protested to Libya about the growing security threat posed by the lawlessness in the region.

There was growing and persistent evidence that ships containing arms and ammunition were plying between the Libyan ports of Misrata and Benghazi and ports in Turkey adjacent to Syria. These shipments were either made with the tacit agreement or the acquiescence of the Libyan government.

Those who advocate dialogue with the Islamic extremists may have found little enthusiasm for their position in Libya's eastern neighbour, Egypt, which was fighting a bloody war in Sinai. According to Egyptian government figures, more than 500 people, most of them military and security forces personnel, were killed across Egypt in militant attacks. The extreme Islamist group Ansar Bayt al-Maqdes claimed responsibility for many of these attacks. Ansar Bayt al-Maqdes hoped to establish a province of the Islamic State in the Sinai Peninsula. Should this happen, Egypt would be threatened by IS/ISIS on its eastern and western flanks. Arms were also moving illegally towards an escalating rebellion in the Sinai where the Egyptian army was waging a war that was likely to attract al-Qaeda franchises and to destabilise the border with Israel. Hezbollah in the Gaza strip was seen to display arms which had their origin in Libya and which it may have been using in its activities in Syria. The Egyptian military was disconcerted about the distribution of Libyan arms among discontented groups west of Suez.

Libya's Prime Minister Kidnapped

On 5 October 2013, the US Delta Force captured al-Qaeda operative Nazih Abdul-Hamed Nabih al-Ruqai'i, whose *nom de guerre* was Abu Anas al-Libi, as he walked home from Friday prayers in the Nufleen district of Tripoli. He was smuggled aboard a US Navy vessel, from whence he was transported to the USA to stand trial for terrorist activities. The Nufleen district was at this point under the control of the Zintan Brigade, the strongest militia in the city. The Libyan Prime Minister, Ali Zeidan, stated that he was unaware that the US were going to carry out the capture.

Whilst this daring operation allowed the Obama administration to claim some much-needed kudos at home, it implied what everyone inside Libya already knew: that the Libyan government had lost control of state security. At the same time, it appeared to be in the pocket of the USA. The combined effect further diminished the authority of the government in some quarters and gave its enemies a propaganda coup.

Then, early on 10 October 2013, the *Libya Herald* carried this startling report:

Dr. Zeidan, the Libyan Prime Minister, was abducted by two gunmen from his room in a Tripoli hotel at around 03.30 this morning. It seems that his bodyguard failed to resist being under the impression that the abduction was official.

Later that day the same paper published this:

The Prime Minister was not released by his captors following negotiations with them, according to government spokesman Mohamed Yahya Kaabar: he was rescued after the headquarters in Fornaj of the Counter Crime Agency was stormed. This version of events was confirmed by Haitham Tajouri, the Commander of the First Support Brigade who had been involved in trying to negotiate Ali Zeidan's freedom. He has said that Ali Zeidan was freed after *thuwwar* from Fornaj and elsewhere in Tripoli had stormed the place where he was held.

It is clear now that local residents of the Fornaj district joined the two *thuwwars*, the First Support Brigade and the 106 Brigade, in storming the building in which the Prime Minster was incarcerated. Ali Zeidan was still, it seems, in his night attire when he was rescued. It is also reported that the powerful Zintan Brigade made it clear that they would 'flatten' the armed groups involved in the kidnap if the Prime Minister was not released – a not inconsiderable threat.

The Egyptian *Asharq Al-Awsat* reported:

The audacious abduction of the Libyan premier by some gunmen on Thursday points to a dangerous state of security instability in the North African country. Speaking exclusively to Asharq Al-Awsat, head of Tripoli's Supreme Security Committee, Hashim Bishr, said that a group affiliated with the Operations Room of Libya's Revolutionaries (ORLR) appeared at the Corinthia

Hotel where Zeidan was staying, informing the prime minister's security guards they had orders from the Public Prosecutor to arrest Zeidan. But Bishr said that Zeidan's guards 'did not see any arrest order.' Tasked with providing security for the Libyan capital, the ORLR 'told him [Zeidan] that he was wanted for questioning and he went with them, although his guards wanted to resist.'

The ORLR was a *thuwwar* or militia which was contracted to the Interior Ministry to provide security in Tripoli. It had no training in police or security work. Its militiamen owed their loyalty to their commanders, not to the state. On the morning of 10 October it stated on its Facebook page that it had been under orders from the Libyan Public Prosecutor when it arrested Ali Zeidan. It later removed this post and began to claim that it had arrested Ali Zeidan on charges of corruption and incompetence and for colluding with the USA in the capture of al-Libi.

Haftar's Operation Dignity

The effect of this chaos in Libya was alarming its neighbours. The southern borders had always been long and difficult to guard – now they became open. Dissident groups from neighbouring countries found the sparsely populated south a useful hiding place. Ghaddafi's armouries had been looted by militias and arms smugglers – to get an idea of the amount involved, there was probably more than the British Army could call on, and some was sophisticated. So Haftar began actively courting allies. Of course, the governments of Libya's neighbours were unable to ally themselves openly with Haftar, but he was still able to make useful contacts who might lobby for him.

On 14 February 2014, Major General Khalifa Haftar released a video in which he stated that 'the national command of the

Libyan Army is declaring a movement for a new road map' to rescue Libya. His plan was to open a campaign in Benghazi and support his allies in Tripoli to rid both cities of Islamist militias. His next objective was Derna. He must have hoped for a quick victory which would allow him to attract more support and resources to allow him to pacify the south, secure the oilfields and expel dissident groups hiding in the Badlands. In May 2014, his forces were gathering for an armed confrontation with Islamist militias in Benghazi; he codenamed it Operation Dignity. In the meantime, the price of Brent crude shot up at the likelihood of a civil war in Libya and the US again moved 600 marines from Spain to a forward base in Sicily in order to protect and evacuate US diplomats and other citizens from Tripoli where Islamist militias ranged freely. They were threatened mainly by powerful forces from Zintan, the city on the edge of the Western Mountains. The Libyan General National Congress, by now probably without legitimate mandate, was attacked by Zintani militias and was stood down. The legitimate but so far ineffective Libyan Army seemed divided and had not shown its hand. The Libyan Air Force units in Tobruk and Benina declared their support for Haftar.

Haftar's forces, now named the Libyan National Army, were based to the east of Benghazi and were said to number 6,000 by 17 May. The Special Service (Lightning) Brigade stationed within the city was reported to have sided with Haftar, who also had tribal support, though the extent of this remains unknown to date. Haftar made his case in a TV broadcast in which he stated that he intended to cleanse and purify Benghazi of militant strife.

The commander-in-chief of Libya's Air Force, Col Gomaa Al-Abbani, said, 'The Air Force's Chief of Staff announces its full accession to Operation Dignity' and called on the Libyan people to 'support the armed forces in their battle against terrorism and to restore security'. In the meantime, political support for the operation appeared. There were reports that the largest political bloc in the Libyan General National Congress, the National Forces Alliance, had voiced its support for Haftar.

Haftar's tribal militiamen began to set up a ring of roadblocks around Benghazi in order to stop Islamist forces, from Derna in particular, from entering the city and coming to the aid of those within. In Benghazi, the Islamist forces made up of the Ansar Sharia Brigade, Libya Shield No. 1, Rafallah al-Sahati Brigade and 17 February Brigade awaited his attention.

Haftar delayed his attack because the Islamist brigades were embedded among the civilian population. His forces needed to prepare for urban warfare, for which special training is needed. There is something especially horrible about urban warfare today. Urban environments with dense populations, narrow streets and multi-storey buildings that serve as enemy defensive positions as they did in Benghazi were challenging for attacking forces. A multi-storey building may take up the same surface area as a small field, but each story or floor contains approximately an equal area as the ground upon which it sits. In effect, a ten-storey building can have eleven times more defensible area than the ground it stands on – ten floors and the flat roof. Buildings and other urban structures, damaged but not destroyed, can be effective cover and provide opportunities for booby traps. Roof areas are excellent locations for snipers or for firing lightweight, handheld anti-tank weapons or MANPADS against attacking aircraft. Underground areas such as sewers, drainage systems and cellars make life difficult for attackers. Both attacker and defender can use these to gain surprise and to conduct ambushes. Defending forces can exploit collateral damage of loss of civilian life as propaganda.

Haftar was now ready, and hopefully about to assert that he was the sole leader capable of dealing with the Salafist-jihadist threat and of taming the numerous and heavily armed militias which dominated the civil powers throughout Libya. Haftar must now take Benghazi and Derna or fail terminally. He could but hope that the Zintani allies would beat the Misratans in Tripoli but he could afford to let that battle take its course and hope that Tripoli folk became angry about their miserable lives and turned to him in desperation, in which case he would be handed Tripoli with a minimum of fighting. He was not at home on the glamorous and rapidly moving battlefield but he had vision and was a talented overall commander, able to delegate and to plan intelligently and meticulously.

He will have asked himself what he wanted to do when he had control of Benghazi and Derna, and sketched out the bare bones of a long-term plan. He then would have built up a talented staff to give his plans substance, commenced a propaganda campaign, secured powerful foreign allies for financial, logistical, air and naval support, built up the coalition he called the Libyan National Army by absorbing militias, mercenaries and regular army units into his fold, set up a recruiting and training command and looked to aiding the civil power after the war. He sought to entice powerful tribal leaders into his fold, find and promote able fighting commanders and to gain political legitimacy. There were few people who could do all that, especially in Libya. But he backed himself to achieve this and probably more.

By the time Haftar was ready to launch his campaign, Libya was in peril – not just in a political sense but moral as well. When moral leadership, law and order and civic society is absent, people tend to seek mutual security by bonding in groups which may be religious, racial, political, tribal, gang or clan. When this happens, individual identity merges with the 'group self' and loathing for other groups is increased. Groups with strong internal identities, especially religious and political ones, become capable of inhuman savagery.

Once they have renounced their individuality and merged with the group self, and if their leaders tell them it is acceptable, eventually people will do savage things. Examples of this are found in the Red Terror, the Cambodian Genocide and the horrors perpetrated in the name of religion today. When religion in particular is infused into the 'group self' it seems to heighten hatred for those who hold incompatible values. The fate of Christians in the Middle East is a notable example. Salafist-Jihadists have begun to see themselves as the sole arbiters of Islam. They persuade their foot-soldiers that 'their hands are prepared to do the blessed act' of beheading their enemies.

Revenge, which is a strong value in Arab culture, may play a part in perpetuating the savagery. The Bedouin tribal concept of '*Amara dam*' – 'those who have agreed on the blood' – refers to a group of close male tribal relatives who are bound to avenge the killing of one of their number or to pay blood money should one of their number kill a member of another tribe. This is a manifestation of group behaviour sanctioned by tradition and which grew up in the lawless and nomadic tribal life of true Arabs.

In Libya, special circumstances existed after the death of Muammar Ghaddafi and Islamist militias exploited them. They were prone to kill and torture in the name of religion – and they were not alone. There were plenty of killers in Libya with different motivations, among them greed and corruption. It is those who kill for one or both – and they are sometimes combined – with whom Khalifa Haftar was, ostensibly, at war. The role that religion will play in Libya's future makes the story of its emergence in the ambitions of powerfully armed militias essential reading.

The militias drained away the tribal loyalties which had helped to bind people together for mutual support, arbitrated in disputes and offered behavioural norms by which people could measure their lives. Militias imposed themselves by force of arms and crashed through the social fabric. They began to dominate and control local government, law enforcement, the judiciary and even the supply of essential services. Do they leave room in Libya for tribal loyalties?

The events in Benghazi, Derna and the south after the fall of Ghaddafi are examples that led Khalifa Haftar to recruit, train, finance and arm his Libyan National Army and to launch it westwards to the gates of Tripoli. There are other incidents which would serve as well or better, but they were the most prominent when Haftar broadcast his ambitions in an address to the nation on 14 February 2014. There are those who saw his announcement on that day as an attempted coup and his subsequent failure to act as a humiliation. While not dismissing the charge of personal ambition so often levied at him, I suggest that there were real and urgent reasons for his announcement – though it proved to be premature.

Because Haftar's campaign was essentially centred in East Libya, the story would seem particularly localised. East Libya – Cyrenaica to many and Barka to a few – has always been a different country. East Libya is Arab in sentiment and attitude whereas West Libya is of the Maghreb and looks westwards. The south has always looked to the Sahel from which it is only divided by an arbitrary frontier, as we have seen in the case of Chad.

When Libya was created in something of a hurry in 1951, the three provinces buried their differences and made an effort to meld into one country. It became, at first, a federal monarchy. Later, in order to accommodate the oil bonanza, it became a unified monarchy so as to ensure the fair distribution of the wealth despite the locations of the oilfields. If we are to discuss the future of Libya, we must rehearse these issues. The likelihood that they will influence Libya's future is strong.

Many who write about Haftar take sides. He is a divisive character – that is true – but we need to step back a little and look at the growth of Islamic extremism and the arrival of the Islamic State in Libya before we rush to conclusions. The story is gruesome and echoes those brutal images which invaded our peaceful living rooms on our TV screens at the time. While following it we may begin to make a more informed judgment of Haftar.

7

CAN HAFTAR SURVIVE?

A Brutal Failure – Islamic State in Libya

Haftar's prime objective was the removal of Islamic jihadist militias from Benghazi and then from Derna. But who were these militias, and to whom or what did they owe their loyalty? Were they affiliated to the big guns such as the Islamic State or al-Qaeda?

Since the eleventh century, the nomadic and semi-nomadic Bedouin tribes of Libya had lived out their traditional lives, moving their tents and animals about their homelands according to the seasons. The Libyan Desert and the Sahara are reluctant to yield food and water to those who choose to live in them, so Libyan tribes took great pains to protect their water sources, their plough land, their seasonal grazing lands and their date palms. They won a frugal living from a harsh environment with which they remained in a finely balanced equilibrium. Consequently, the appearance of strangers in their homelands was treated with a degree of the suspicion which underlay their traditional desert hospitality. The Bedouin humour needs a practised ear to appreciate it, but you can hear it in the phrase they use when strangers overstay their welcome: 'The camel's nose is in the tent.'

The Islamic State had its nose in Libya's tent. The group had been formed around the late Abu Musab al-Zarqawi, a Jordanian whose methods became too extreme for al-Qaeda and from which he split to form his own group. But despite its alarming reputation for the ruthless and rapid exploitation of much of Iraq and Syria, Islamic State experienced some unexpected barriers to its expansion in Libya. There were four main reasons for this. Firstly, there was no Sunni–Shia sectarian divide which it could exploit in Libya as it had done with success in Iraq. Secondly, the ancient and powerful Libyan tribes proved resistant to its blandishments. Thirdly, and perhaps crucially, it had not been able to get its hands on some of the oil revenue. Finally, as a latecomer, it had made poor progress against the numerous powerful Libyan militias which had their own powerbases and ambitions. In particular, the Islamic State in Derna, and later Sirte, was in competition with the militant Islamist group Ansar al-Sharia, which was currently under attack by the Libyan National Army in nearby Benghazi.

Ansar al-Sharia in Libya was formed in June 2012 as a coalition of East Libyan militias mainly from Benghazi led by a sometime inmate of Ghaddafi's notorious Abu Salim gaol called Mohammad al-Zawahi. As we have seen, the group had been accused of killing the US ambassador Chris Stevens. Its members courted public support by establishing cultural centres in cities and sought to fill the security gap by acting as traffic cops and street cleaners. Its funding appeared to arise from donations as there were few stories of protection money in circulation. Its uncompromising application and advocacy of Sharia Law and the proclamation of local caliphates in Benghazi and Derna led to suspicions that it was linked to the Islamic State or al-Qaeda in the Islamic Maghreb. It is more likely that it demonstrated its Libyan characteristics by remaining localised, though it remained sympathetic to the big guns. There were so called 'branches' of the franchise in Tunisia and elsewhere, and it may have formed alliances of convenience with other Islamist groups, though not for long.

In April 2014, reports emanated from Derna, where Khalifa Haftar had attended school, that the gang calling itself the Islamic State was murdering members of prominent families in a bid to retain control of the town with a show of ruthless brutality. An horrific photograph circulated on the internet showing the dead and brutalised bodies of three men hung by their wrists in a simulated crucifixion. The victims were said to be members of the Harir al-Mansouri family, one of several local families who had met to plan a way of eliminating the IS gang and which had several subsequent armed clashes. The Islamic State leadership in the town was clearly rattled.

Then, in June, the group declared the establishment of a Libyan caliphate – defined broadly as a state governed under strict Sharia law by a caliph who is God's deputy on Earth. It demanded that Muslims swear allegiance to its then leader – Ibrahim Awad Ibrahim al-Badri al-Samarrai, better known as Abu Bakr al-Baghdadi, who was based in Iraq and Syria. It required other jihadist groups to acknowledge and accept its supreme authority.

This move followed a visit by fifteen members of Islamic State, led by an Egyptian and a Saudi national, who travelled to Derna from Syria. Hundreds of IS veterans, known as the Battar Group or Brigade, who had been fighting in Deir Ezzour in eastern Syria and Mosul in northern Iraq, also decamped to Derna. In September, a Yemeni militant arrived from Syria to become their leader. Ansar al-Sharia and its allies declared Derna the *Whilaya Barca fil ad-Dawlah al-Islām* – that is the 'Provence of Cyrenaica within the Islamic State'. For them this meant that the city was no longer a part of Libya but owed its allegiance to the brutal caliphate led by Abu Bakr al-Baghdadi.

There are good and scholarly papers about militant Islam in Libya which point out that the city of Derna supplied an unusually high number of fighters against both the Russian and US military in Afghanistan. Indeed, analysts and journalists highlight Derna as an intellectual and spiritual hub of militant Islamists, and my observations support their conclusions. That the Islamic State in Iraq and Syria, looking as it was for an alternative venue for its caliphate, saw Derna as a strong contender is no surprise. But why?

If you approach Derna by road down the notable Z bends from the Green Mountains and see the city below you on the shore of the Libyan Sea, you may be struck – as I was in the 1960s – by its benign isolation. In those days there were still some remnants of the Italian colonial architecture but the predominant culture was profoundly Islamic. There were few, if any, women to be seen and my wife always felt uneasy if she accompanied me. Young men in the city had few outlets for their energies except those provided by the mosques. Imams tended to frown upon recreational sport, and especially on the diversions available to Western youths, as un-Islamic. By the 1980s male youths were deprived of outlets for their energies. While Khalifa Haftar attended school in the city, the was little education available for the majority of young adolescents outside the mosques.

The Senussi sect had been strong in Derna and Omar al-Mukhtar, its hero, was born not too far away. He was a member of the Minifa tribe. The Minifa is a client tribe of the al-Obaidat, which dominates the region. Omar al-Mukhtar led the fight against the Christian Italian colonists from 1911, so the tradition of jihad, the outward aspect of the obligation to fight the enemies of Islam, was deeply entrenched in Derna.

Male youths were limited in their social lives, and their heroes – both the legendry Omar al-Mukhtar and the modern fighters who had returned from fighting the Russians with the Mujahideen in Afghanistan in the 1980s – were jihadists. A potent mix of male peer bonding and militant Islamic heroism then made the young men easy pickings for jihadist recruiters in the fight against the US in Iraq and Assad in Syria. Later, there were numerous and ready recruits for the anti-Ghaddafi *thuwwars* and, after he was eliminated by the Islamist militias in Derna, Benghazi and elsewhere for the militias which fought against each other and attempted to rule the notably peaceable Muslims of Libya's east.

IS had easily been able to make a lodgement in Sirte, which was remote from the political powers centred in Tripoli and Tobruk. I have emphasised the problems that long distances pose for military planners in Libya. Both Derna and Sirte were attractive to IS because of the distance military forces from Benghazi and Tripoli would have to cover to attack them. To do so would require a considerable logistical effort so that an attacking force did not run out fuel and ammunition.

The Islamic State gained complete control of the coastal city of Sirte and its neighbouring town of Al-Nawfaliyah. Sirte was Ghaddafi's hometown and he had poured a great deal of money into it. He was killed trying to escape from it in 2011 and the city had been a pariah ever since. It was thus virtually lawless and an easy target for IS. Some say, only partly in jest, that no one else wanted it. It lay between the de facto government based in Tripoli and the internationally recognised government based in the eastern city of Tobruk. These 'governments' were so badly at odds that they were unable to combine to root IS out of Sirte, leaving its militants safe until of the governments raised sufficient force to attack and eliminate it.

If you make the journey from Tripoli to Benghazi by road, the Tripoli oasis ends as the road turns south-east at Misrata. From there it dives into the desert, through which it continues with little interruption but for the towns and oil ports for more than 650 kilometres until it reaches Ajdabiya. It is hard to convey in a few words how daunting that desert journey was when I made it in the mid-twentieth century. It is somewhat easier now, but it is clear how difficult it would be to mount an attack on IS in its stronghold in Sirte. So safe did IS feel that it is from there that it operated its own satellite TV station, Al-Bayan, on which it broadcast its propaganda. Much of this material exaggerated the actual strength of IS in Libya and it failed to point out that most of its fighters were foreign. It also bore the classic hallmarks of its methods in Iraq in that it proclaimed three caliphates in Libya: one in each of the historic provinces of Cyrenaica, Tripolitania and the Fezzan. The latter two consisted of very few adherents who were nonetheless involved in acts of terrorism. This terrified people, as it was intended to do.

The IS lodgement in Sirte posed a severe threat to Libya's oil crescent, especially if IS were to bracket it and take, and maintain, control of Ajdabiya or otherwise foray out of its strongholds in quick raids to cut the crude oil pipelines. This concentrated minds marvellously as, if it did so, the whole IS camel would be inside the tent, not just its nose. Eyewitness reports gleaned from social media at the time show similar trends to those experienced at the hands of militant Islamists in Benghazi – that is, they spread alarm and fear by murdering prominent citizens.

This from my blog Libyastories.com. A Salafist imam was murdered in Ajdabiya when a car bomb exploded beneath his vehicle. Ten days earlier the local army intelligence chief Colonel Ataya Al-Arabi died in a hail of gunfire as he drove up to his home. The day before that there was an attempt to kill another Salafist imam in the town in a similar car bomb attack. He escaped serious injury but his nephew was killed. Hassuna Al-Atawish Al-Magharbi, the commander of the LNA's Brigade 302, which was fighting in Benghazi, was shot dead in the town. Local militiaman Nasser Al-Rugaieh and political activist Belgassem Al-Zwai were killed in separate incidents and there was an attempt to kill local journalist Usama Al-Jarred. Almost all the attacks were blamed on the Islamist Ajdabiya Revolutionaries' Shoura Council. This is a local group.

In Derna the teaching of foreign languages, mathematics and science was banned and the local higher education institute and the law department at the town's Omar al-Mukhtar University was closed – the latter because it was not teaching Sharia law, the former because of gender mixing among staff and students. The Derna Caliphate had also imported foreign judges, one of whom was from the Yemen, said to be versed in Sharia law to preside over new courts. Some youths caught drinking alcohol were sentenced to be lashed with palm branches stripped of their leaves in the courtyard of an old mosque.

It was notable that both IS lodgements avoided a major confrontation from either of Libya's rival governments. This is possibly just as well. That it met any resistance to its expansion in Libya may have been the reason for its notable brutality in Derna and also for the publication of a video of its execution of thirty Ethiopian Christians in two locations in East and South Libya, two months after it beheaded twenty-one Egyptian Copts. A video of this last event showed the Copts dressed in orange jumpsuits as worn by inmates of the US detention centre at Guantanamo Bay. They were marched to a beach and forced to kneel. Before the killings, one of the militants stood with a knife in his hand and said, 'Safety for you crusaders is something you can only wish for.'

This rhetoric, directed at Arab Christians, was clearly intended to imply that the Islamic State had managed to expand in Libya from its limited presence in the eastern towns of Derna and Sirte. It declared that Libya was already in their power. In the long run, the side effect of this gruesome video was to make the Egyptian government very angry indeed, as the Egyptian Copts were numerous and influential and undergoing persecution in Egypt. It reacted almost immediately. The Egyptian Air Force bombed Islamic State targets inside Derna. It was the first time Egypt confirmed launching air strikes against the group in neighbouring

Libya, showing they were ready to expand their own fight against Islamist militancy beyond their borders. The targets of the dawn strike, in which Libya's air force also participated, hit IS camps, training sites and weapons storage areas.

The West had much to fear from Islamic State attempting to infiltrate the throngs of migrants crossing the Mediterranean from Libya in order to export ruthless terrorists to Europe's vulnerable cities. However, there was another threat which needed attention. That was the potential for the Islamic State's exploitation of the lawless southern regions of Libya. The south is home to the oilfields are and the fossil water aquifers. These regions, bordering on the Sudan, Chad, Niger, Mali and Algeria, would offer a haven for IS and allow it to exercise a perceived influence far in excess of its real power. Should its members fetch up there, they would find a source of revenue in the trafficking of drugs, arms and people. They would also be able to exploit the unrest among the Tuaregs, and to this end they began to post propaganda in Tamahaq. Once established in South Libya, the Islamic State could threaten to mount attacks on the Algerian natural gas complex, Libyan oil installations and the Nigerian yellow cake uranium mines.

There were growing fears of a connection between Libyan Islamists and ISIS in Iraq, al-Qaeda in the Islamic Maghreb, Al-Shabaab in Somalia and Kenya and Boko Haram in Nigeria. Thus far, the main reason for optimism lay in the fractious nature of these Islamist jihadists groups. For example, one of the reasons IS had not so far appeared in strength in South Libya was that the region was within the bailiwick of a legendary war lord – Mokhtar Belmokhtar, also known as Khaled Abou El Abbas or Laaouar – who was an Algerian terrorist of the mid-Saharan Arab Chaamba tribe, leader of the group Al-Murabitoun, sometime al-Qaeda emir and kidnapper, smuggler and weapons dealer. Belmokhtar had been reported dead so many times that he was thought to be indestructible. (He is finally said to have been killed in Ajdabiya during a meeting in 2015.)

Haftar Wins Benghazi and Derna after a Long and Bitter Struggle

While IS was taking hold in Derna, on 16 May 2014 Khalifa Haftar launched his National Libya Army against the Islamist militias which had for some time dominated the citizens of Benghazi. These militias, the Ansar al-Sharia Brigade, Libya Shield No. 1, Rafallah al-Sahati Brigade and 17th February Brigade, had espoused a doctrinal form of Islam called Salafism. Recently there were signs of a more extreme form of this doctrine surfacing in the city called Takfirism. Takfiris reject any reform or change to their interpretation of religion as it was revealed in the time of the prophet. Those who deny the fundamental foundations of Islam, or follow any other form of Islam, they call apostates and regard as non-Muslims.

The *Libya Herald* dated 17 May reported:

> Haftar launched his assault [on 16 May] on Ansar Sharia as well as on 17 February Brigade and Libya Shield No. 1 Brigade, both widely viewed in the city as Islamist, from his Al-Rajma military compound in the east of the city yesterday morning. The operation which took everyone by surprise has so far left dozens dead and at least 250 wounded. Benghazi Medical Centre told the *Libya Herald* that it had 35 bodies and dealt with 138 injury cases. Jalaa Hospital said it had two dead and 29 injured and Marj Hospital six dead and 81 injured.

Haftar's forces were still in armed confrontation with Islamist militias in Benghazi when he declared that his forces would soon be in Tripoli and that his intention was to rid Libya of Islamist militias and their supporters, some of whom, he claimed, were foreign. In particular, he singled out the Muslim Brotherhood as his main 'political' target.

The wider effects of his announcements forced Libya's immediate neighbours, Tunisia and Algeria to the west and Egypt to the east, to engage in an assessment of his strengths and weaknesses and move military resources to contain any spill-over should Libya disintegrate into total chaos and become a Somalia on the Mediterranean. All these states have their own issues with Islamists. On 29 May, Egypt elected the former military chief Abdul Fattah al-Sisi as president after a turbulent period of – admittedly democratically elected – Islamist government, and was engaged in an ongoing low-grade war with jihadists in Sinai. The stakes were high. If Libya became a stronghold for al-Qaeda and Salafist-jihadists the stability of much of North Africa would be threatened. Haftar's attack on Benghazi, therefore, mattered, and his actions and ambitions would be criticised and questioned.

At the time of Haftar's attack on Benghazi, the coastal city of Derna was firmly in Islamist hands and the vast and lawless south of Libya was a haven for al-Qaeda franchises and criminals. The coalition which had attempted to govern post-Ghaddafi Libya had disintegrated and there were two prime ministers, neither of whom could deal with the serious security problems. Haftar was attempting to demonstrate that only he could deal with the growing anarchy. Did he have political ambitions? We know he stated that he was willing to run the country if that was the popular demand.

The battle lines in Libya were now clear. Remember that Ansar al-Sharia had issued this uncompromising statement:

The goal of Ansar al-Sharia brigade is to implement the laws of Allah on the land, and reject the human implemented laws and earthly made constitutions. There will be nothing ruling in this country other than the laws of Allah.

As Haftar's warplanes bombed his strongholds in Benghazi, a defiant Ansar al-Sharia military commander, Mohammed

Al-Zahawi, accused him of waging a crusade against Islam. He portrayed Haftar's forces as lackeys of the US, Saudi Arabia, the UAE and Egypt and warned him that he would suffer the same fate as Ghaddafi. Zahawi later asserted that his forces beat off the attack launched on Benghazi by Haftar on 16 May and claimed it as a victory for Ansar al-Sharia:

> We thank God that we were able to defeat Haftar and we challenge him to attempt entering Benghazi again. We warn him that if he continues this war against us, Muslims from across the world will come to fight, as is the case in Syria right now.

But Haftar had positioned himself as the sole leader capable of dealing with the Salafist-jihadist threat and taming the numerous and heavily armed militias which dominated the civil powers throughout Libya. His task was to gather support from the Libyan man in the street, and he claimed that demonstrations in his favour in Benghazi and Tripoli gave him a popular mandate. A pro-Haftar demonstration outside Benghazi's Tibesti Hotel was, however, countered by another, albeit much smaller one, in Tahrir Square. In an interview published in *Asharq al-Awsat* on 22 May 2014, Haftar was quoted as saying,

> The security problem is a major issue that has shaken our country in a frightening manner after the General National Council allowed all the terrorist forces across the world to come to Libya and coexist with the Libyan people. We know that these terrorists can never coexist with the people of Libya. The Muslim Brotherhood is leading this move. They are being granted Libyan passports and are coming to our country from abroad. There is now a large group of Brothers here, and that is why our neighbours are raising questions about this situation – particularly Egypt, Algeria and Tunisia. These groups, unfortunately, represent a great threat.

Haftar argued that tribal and ethnic discord needed urgent attention. The Cyrenaican Federalists were still in control of the main oil terminals and the unruly south presented a military problem of its own. The Russians quickly made a diplomatic move by favouring one of the two rival Libyan prime ministers. On the matter of popular support, on 1 June the *Libya Herald* said,

> Haftar claimed ... that popular support had provided him a mandate to continue his campaign against militant Islamist groups ... Others saw no difference between the illegitimate Haftar, who they saw as pursuing his own personal political agenda, and the extremist militias he was confronting.

It was not just popular support that Haftar cultivated, but tribal support. This is an interesting paradox in his personality: his military leadership style could alienate, but his ability to conduct negotiations among the tribes was well proven. Benghazi is within the homeland of the Awaquir tribe, which has a number of leading families and is thus not always consistent in its loyalties. Haftar managed his relationship with this tribe effectively but in return it expected privileged access to influence in the city.

When he moved on to take Derna in 2014, it was the Obeiadt tribe whose cooperation and participation Haftar had to encourage. He had not yet achieved the personal loyalty of some of the participating militias, and the force which he launched against Derna was a coalition. Among it were some citizens bent on revenge.

Islamic State Is Ousted

The Islamic State outlived its welcome. Sometime in early July 2015, an IS preacher at a Derna mosque stated that IS supporters were the only true Muslims. He declared all other Islamist militias in Derna *murtad* or, in English, apostate. In this he revealed the true Takfiri nature of IS and its franchises. The rival Islamist grouping, the Shoura Council of Mujahideen formed in Derna a few months earlier to oppose Haftar, immediately issued an ultimatum telling IS to renounce Takfiri extremism and to stop its brutal murders or face the consequences.

The Mujahideen consisted at that time of four Islamic militias: Ansar al-Sharia in Derna, headed by Sufian Ben Qumu; the Abu Saleem Martyrs' Brigade, headed by Salem Derbi; the Islamic Army, headed by Amin Kalfa; and the Islamic Fighting Group, headed by Nasser Akkar. It expelled the Islamic State from Derna, whereupon IS members took refuge in Ras Hilal in the Green Mountains and clashed with units of the Libyan National Army.

The presence of IS could also no longer be tolerated in Sirte. In April 2016, Haftar made a move against it at the same time as the Misratans launched an attack from the west accompanied by British and Italian special forces and supported by US air power. Haftar's part in Operation Bunyan Massous, as the Misratans named it, has been overlooked. The possibility that IS might escape to the east had to be anticipated and blocked, and Haftar was further from Sirte than the Misratans so he had to send his blocking force a long way to be effective.

Haftar planned to approach Sirte from the east with his Libyan National Army and to send another irregular force around to its south-west. For their part, the Misratans were to move eastwards towards Sirte by a conventional route along the 200-kilometre coastal road. Haftar's forces of around 1,000, equipped with some armed personnel carriers and the ubiquitous pickups supplied by the United Arab Emirates, advanced eastwards from his base east of Benghazi. In support, Haftar appointed Colonel Idris Mahdi to lead Colonel Mohmad Ben Nail's 241 Brigade, who were nearer Sirte at the time, and Colonel al-Seedi al-Tabawey's 25 Brigade, all of whom were Tebu, to approach from the south-west. Haftar, with an eye on history and propaganda, gave this blocking move the codename Operation Qurdabiya 2 to commemorate the battle against the Italians in 1915, unique as the only time when Tripolitanian, Fezzani and Cyrenaican forces have fought together.

The battle started on 19 May 2016 and ended – after considerable loss of life and the near-total destruction of much of the city – on 10 December. Among the IS fighters killed in the action, three were British. At the time the British public was disturbed by the presence in Iraq of a notorious IS executioner dubbed Jihadi John who flaunted his ruthless talent for beheading people on social media.

The Siege on Derna

While the battle for Sirte was still ongoing, in August 2016, Haftar's forces placed Derna under siege. After the summary execution of the pilot of one of Haftar's aircraft, shot down when attacking DRSC positions, the siege was tightened and residents began to run short of food and medical supplies. There was an inaccurate bombing raid on the city which caused collateral damage and civilian deaths. The raid was attributed to, but denied by, Egypt. These events drew international condemnation which may have damaged Haftar, not least because they caused hesitation on the part of the Egyptians to continue their overt support. The United Nations Mission in Libya reminded Haftar 'that direct or indiscriminate attacks against civilians are prohibited under international humanitarian law and reminds all parties of their obligations to protect civilians'.

Ranged against him in the increasingly important propaganda war was Libya's hard-line Grand Mufti Sheik Sadiq al-Ghariani, who was based in Tripoli and had his own TV station from whence he preached throughout Libya. He was unassailable and strongly supporting of Salafist-jihadist organisations in East Libya. By now Haftar had strengthened his propaganda arm, which had plenty of competition. His enemies were adept at going for his weakness, calling him a self-styled field marshal, a war lord, a failure at Ouadi Doum, and a renegade. These tags appeared in the international press.

Derna and Al-Abyar – Haftar's Hostages to Fortune?

Haftar had opened hostilities in Benghazi in May 2014. The battle for the city lasted until July 2017, when the city returned to some sort of normality. But it had been brutal. Many were killed, much damage to property was caused and numerous people displaced. His next major objective, Derna, was finally cleared of the last remaining Islamists in 2018. Derna, too, had been a difficult nut to crack and Haftar's campaign to take the city has left him with human rights issues.

A Human Rights Watch report tells us that a video of a mass execution was posted on social media on 24 July 2017 in which a Colonel al-Werfalli and some LNA soldiers were seen wearing the insignia of the Army Special Forces. Colonel Al-Werfalli read out an execution judgment, identified the unit, the date of 17 July, and the capital offences attributed to a number of men in custody. He was then seen as the main executioner or supervisor of executions in six more video recordings of apparent summary executions of people accused of 'terrorism' and committing crimes against the LNA.[13]

In October 2017, the bodies of thirty-six men were found in Al-Abyar, east of Benghazi. Bearing signs of torture and gunshot wounds to the head, they were said to be the bodies of militant fighters who had for so long held out against Haftar's soldiers. The suspicion was growing that a Libyan National Army field

---

13. https://www.hrw.org/news/2017/08/16/libya-videos-capture-summary-executions

commander may have been involved in or at least directed the killings. This from Human Rights Watch makes the point clearly:

> Human Rights Watch reviewed seven videos and several still images that appear to show distinct incidents of LNA-affiliated soldiers executing prisoners in their custody. Some of these videos and images show fighters desecrating the bodies of supposed fighters who opposed the LNA, including the burning and kicking of a corpse and posing for photographs with another corpse that had a leash tied around its neck.

On 15 August 2018 the International Criminal Court prosecutor issued an international arrest warrant against LNA special forces commander Mahmoud al-Werfalli, after the emergence of the videos implicating him in the apparent summary executions in eastern Libya of the thirty-six men found in al-Abyar.

More unpleasantness was to come. In social media footage from Derna, dead bodies were seen being toyed with, hung from machine gun turrets and draped over the bucket of an excavation digger. The crimes shown in the videos and photos could also amount to crimes against humanity. Human Rights Watch urged the international community to investigate the commanders, including Haftar, for potentially ordering and directing the violations, or for failing in their duties to effectively prevent or punish the crimes committed by their subordinates. 'It is a crime against humanity if it can be established on all the evidence that they were committed as part of a widespread or systematic attack directed against the civilian population of Derna,' the report reads. 'The investigation and prosecution of those up the chain of command is very important in order to establish the full record of criminal activity, to guarantee accountability and justice, and to deter the future occurrence of similar crimes in the conflict.'

A point worthy of note in this regard is that the heaviest clusters of 'conflict-related mortality' during the period from 2012 to 2017 were to be found in Derna and Benghazi followed by Sirte.[14] I argue that civilians faced the brunt of the danger because of economic instability, airstrikes and artillery shelling, displacement, exploitation and abuse. The effect on the mental health of the civilian population caused by the protracted conflict, in which torture and brutality were and remain commonplace, is unquantifiable and likely to echo down the generations. Whatever his record on human rights contraventions, Haftar must face the accusations which arise from the conflict, as he was in overall command. That must include those made against militias fighting in cooperation with the LNA.

Field Marshal Khalifa Haftar Launches a Bid for Power

On 18 December 2017, British newspaper *The Times* ran a piece on Field Marshal Khalifa Haftar which opened with these words:

> The most powerful military commander in Libya has declared the internationally recognised government redundant and suggested that he should run the country.
>
> In a speech likely to lead to further chaos in the already fractured nation Khalifa Haftar, whose forces control most of east Libya, claimed that a 2015 UN-brokered peace deal had expired, rendering the government that emerged from it illegitimate.
>
> In an address broadcast from his headquarters in Benghazi, General Haftar said: 'All bodies resulting from this agreement automatically lose their legitimacy, which has been contested from the first day they took office.'

---

14. https://journals.plos.org/plosone/article?id=10.1371/journal.
   pone.0216061

Acknowledging that the country was now at an 'historic and dangerous turning point', he hinted that he would consider filling the political void by running for president.

There was an intense diplomatic effort underway to settle Libya's brutal and persistent civil war. Egyptian President Abdul Fattah al-Sisi, who had much to lose if it failed, led the charge. The Gulf States and Tunisia also played prominent roles in the negotiations. The Gulf States had been deeply involved in the hasty intervention which led to Ghaddafi's downfall but which set off a predictable and bloody civil and religious war. For some time it had been apparent that Haftar and his army had been gaining control over much of East Libya and he could no longer be referred to as a 'renegade general'. He was now a major, but strangely divisive, factor to be accounted for if Libya was to have a future. The opposing parties in Libya's armed chaos were weary, as were ordinary Libyans. It was time to sort things out.

What Will Field Marshal Khalifa Haftar Do Next?

In June 2017, Haftar's forces had made a significant strategic move. They took possession of the Brak al-Shatti and Jufra airbases in southern and central Libya, effectively seizing them from the Misratan 13th Brigade and Mustafa Al-Sharksi's Benghazi Defence Brigade, which had deployed ruthless tactics. The 13th Brigade is said to have withdrawn to its base in Misrata and the Benghazi Defence Brigade to Sabratha to the west of Tripoli.

Once Haftar's advance troops had made the airfields safe, cleared their approaches and organised the logistics, he was able to position his warplanes within striking distance of Misrata and Tripoli. He could also use his transport aircraft to ferry in material and reinforcements to build up a strong foothold in central Libya. This shifted Haftar's strategic outlook considerably and gave him a new set of political and tribal considerations peculiar to the south and west of the country.

Let us look at it now from the tribal point of view. Brak al-Shatti is in the territory of the Magraha tribe of Abdulbaset al-Megrahi, the convicted Lockerbie bomber. Notable among the tribe's sons are Abdulla Senussi, Ghaddafi's brother-in-law and sometime intelligence supremo, and Major Abdul Salem Jalloud, Ghaddafi's sometime second-in-command. Jufra is within the tribal homeland of the Awlad Suleiman, to which Ghaddafi's tribe, the Ghaddadfa, is in a client relationship. Both are in the vicinity of Sebha, the acknowledged capital of Libya's old province of the Fezzan.

The modern town of Sebha had developed from the three oasis settlements of Jedid, Quatar and Hejer and now housed a population of around 200,000. It was the seat of the Saif al-Nasr family, the most prominent and revered leaders of the Awlad Sulieman tribe and its historic allies and clients. The Saif al-Nasr family gained heroic status in its wars with their Ottoman Turk overlords in the early nineteenth century and with the Italian colonists in the early twentieth century.

Ghaddafi's father migrated from Sirte to Sebha to take menial employment with the Saif al-Nasr family, something which his son was said to resent. Ghaddafi attended secondary school in Sebha and staged his first anti-government demonstration as a schoolboy in the city. He also held a demonstration in the lobby of a hotel owned by the Saif al-Nasr family, thus ensuring his expulsion from school. The relationship between Sebha and Ghaddafi was ambiguous.

The Saif al-Nasr family and the Awlad Suleiman tribe it led were the dominant force in Sebha and in much of the Fezzan throughout the Ottoman Turkish regency (1551–1911), the Italian colonial period (1911–1943), the short period of French military government after the Second World War (1943–1951) and the Kingdom of Libya (1951–1969). During the forty or so years of the Ghaddafi era, the dominance in the Fezzan of the Awlad Suleiman was reversed in favour of his own tribe, the Ghaddadfa, and that of his closest supporters, the Magraha tribe.

Apart from a number of so-called al-Ahali, the name given to long-time town dwellers, Sebha offered a home to people from other tribes. There were also colonies of the Magraha from the Wadi Shati to the north, the Awlad Abu Seif and the Hasawna tribe who, in the past, were the true nomads of the south and allies of the Awlad Suleiman.

There was one district of Sebha which had been a source of discord for some time. It was the Tauri district, which was colonised by some Tuareg and many Tebu.

Since the fall of Ghaddafi, Tebu militias had come to dominate the south and Libya's borders with Chad and Niger. They were perceived by the majority of the inhabitants of Sebha to be non-Libyans trying to control the city. In particular they now dominated the majority of the trade (legal and illicit) routes between Sebha and the Chad basin. Thus, they had a firm grip on the regional arms and drug trade and on people trafficking. The Awlad Suleiman tribesmen may still have had their own trade routes in this area but perceived the Tebu to be a foreign and ethnically inferior threat to their historic dominance of the region

Powerful Western Tribes

Haftar had allies among the Zintanis in the Western Mountains some 180 kilometres south-west of Tripoli. They had been preparing to move back into Tripoli for some time. They referred to themselves as the Western Command of Haftar's Libyan National Army and were well armed and thirsting for revenge, having been beaten out of Tripoli in the summer of 2014 by the Misratan-led forces. Were Haftar and his Libyan National Army to move towards Tripoli he would likely be joined by his allies from Zintan. To that end he trained a considerable number of new recruits to augment the battle-hardened Zintani militias.

Haftar's relation with the Zintanis was not easy, however. One of his sometime army generals, Usama al-Juwaili, hated him and was highly influential in military circles in the city and held in high regard by many influential Libyans. He was appointed defence minister under the Transitional National Council after Saif al-Islam al-Ghaddafi was captured by a Zintani militia paroling the border with Tunisia. Al-Juwaili controlled the powerful Zintan Military Council and thus challenged Haftar. The reason for the animosity between the two is not clear. Haftar meanwhile sounded out, and likely received support from, the Warishifana tribe whose territory dominated Tripoli's western approaches.

Misrata, Libya's third-largest city and some 210 kilometres east of Tripoli, was in the process of change. The municipal council was beginning to assert itself against the powerful Islamist militias which had dominated the city for some considerable time. The militias were, however, still well armed and Haftar would have been wise to outflank them were he to intend to dominate Tripoli. It was perhaps this consideration which influenced his strategy.

Haftar indicated that his next step was to move some 300 kilometres north-east into Bani Walid. Bani Walid is the stronghold of the Warfella tribe and was one of the last pro-Ghaddafi centres to surrender during the 2011 civil war. The Warfella, one of West Libya's Sa'adi tribes, is also said to be one of Libya's largest and was greatly favoured by Ghaddafi for much of his reign. There were reports that Haftar had already met Warfella leaders to discuss future operations but there were still said to be a number of Ghaddafists in Bani Walid. Which horse would the Bani Walid leaders put their money on?

Haftar Consolidates His Position in Central Libya

On 17 October 2017, Haftar told a meeting of his army commanders in Benghazi that the size of Libya was 1,760,000 square kilometres and that the Libyan National Army he commanded controlled 1,730,000 square kilometres of it.

As expected, he reached an agreement with the Warfella tribe based around Bani Walid. He then raised the new 27th Infantry Brigade for recruits from the Warfella under the command of Colonel Abdulla al-Warfella. The new regiment was scheduled to undergo a period of training but it was clear that Haftar's sphere of influence had been extended to one of Libya's respected tribes with wide territorial influence.

The leadership of the Warfella tribe under Sheikh Mohamad al-Barghouti had notably distanced itself from the armed discord which had bedevilled Libya since the downfall of the Ghaddafi regime. However, they had long been at odds with the Misratans, who had conducted a siege of Bani Walid in 2012 on the pretext of flushing out Ghaddafists who were said to have been afforded refuge there.

What the Field Marshall did not say on 17 October, but his commanders knew, was that he had not reached an accommodation with the militias of Misrata, It was hard to see how he intended to deal with the considerable challenge they posed. Nor did he appear to have addressed the Tuareg militias in the south-west of the country, though he had no doubt entered into discussions with their leaders.

Some observers now believed Haftar was preparing to enter Tripoli. He had a number of tactical problems to overcome, not least that there were some strong but warring militias in Tripoli which would not take readily to the loss of power they currently exercised. They may have put aside their differences and opposed him. He did not wish to confront them in built-up areas and cause collateral damage, and it may be that he was negotiating with people in the city in order to eliminate, or at least reduce, armed opposition.

He may have used the fact that a large proportion of Tripoli's civil population was heartily fed up with the constant armed battles between militias and the shortages of fuel and electricity. For example, the people of Tripoli had recently suffered severe water shortages because the flow of water from the sub-Saharan aquifers in the Jebel Hasouna had been interrupted by an armed gang which attacked the electricity control room supplying the pumps. He would need to block the Misratan militias who would, no doubt, attempt a flanking attack on his forces.

Haftar's Chips Are on the Table; Is It Time to Spin the Wheel?

On 25 October 2017, Haftar's communication chief, Colonel Ahmed Mismari, stated that the Libyan National Army was now preparing to go to Tripoli, where it would be welcomed by the people. He told the press that the 'LNA's new operational area was West Libya', that is the old Province of Tripolitania, and preparations were now in hand for the 'next phase' of what he called the 'decisive battle for the Libyan Army'. He implied that Haftar had given the politicians six months to bring some form of stable and effective government into being before the LNA moved to take over.

Were Haftar and his Libyan National Army truly intending to move towards Tripoli, he would likely have been joined by his allies from Zintan in the Western Mountains. And for the moment, he had clearly allied himself to the Warfella tribe. He was thus in a strong position to the south-east of Tripoli but, as discussed above, threatened by the Misratan militias. However, between the Warfella and the city lies the Tarhuna tribe.

No doubt Haftar's intelligence people had made a thorough assessment of the Tarhuna tribal leadership and its likely allegiances. From the observer's standpoint the outstanding problem with the Tarhuna was the Kani militia which dominated the tribe and had the Tarhuna town council in its pocket. The Kani militia claimed to be Islamist but there were some who observed its operations with scepticism and suggest it had a record of revenge killings and involvement in shady trading. It does seem to have been unscrupulous in practice. Haftar's people would have noted that the Kani militia was allied to the Misratan militias in Operation Libyan Dawn during which Haftar's allies, the Zintanis, were beaten out of Tripoli and wanton destruction of aircraft and property took place at Tripoli's international airport. If Haftar was to dine with the Kani militia he would need a long spoon.

Where Is Khalifa Haftar?

In some Western cultures, Friday 13th is considered unlucky. Perhaps it was an unlucky day for Libya, as on Friday 13 April 2018 reports in the Libyan press and in the UK broadsheet *The Guardian* speculated that Khalifa Haftar had suffered a stroke and was in hospital in Paris. His spokesman denied the reports, but by 24 April the rumours had gathered pace.

Reports of his death were beginning to gain in strength. It was said that Haftar had been transported to the Val-de-Grace military hospital in Paris after falling ill in Jordan, but other sources suggested that he had suffered a severe and debilitating stroke which would require constant ongoing medical attention and render him unfit to rule Libya.

It was supposed that President Sisi of Egypt and leaders in the UAE were working hard to delay official announcements of Haftar's demise because the tensions within the Libyan National Army would otherwise be released with drastic consequences. 'Because he's so revered in eastern Libya, any potential successor to Haftar would likely face serious challenges from within the LNA, and his death could trigger deep internal conflict,' wrote Sarah Al-Shaalan, a Middle East and North Africa researcher at risk consultancy Eurasia Group.

There were suggestions that one of Haftar's two sons would take over. One of them commanded 106 Brigade of the LNA, which was in control of Benghazi. It was reported to have moved by night to Libya's oil crescent. That would make sense in the light of the rising alarm, were it to be true. The possibility that Misratan forces would take the opportunity to move on the oil facilities around the Gulf of Sirte must have crossed the minds of LNA leaders.

Names of potential replacements emerged. The LNA Special Forces commander Wanis Bukhamada had been reassigned to Derna; he had not always seen eye to eye with Haftar. Would he make a bid for power? Haftar's very powerful Chief of Staff, Abdul Razzaq Al-Nadhuri, was head of the Benghazi Joint Security Room (BR). He had recently survived a car bomb attack. Possible tensions between Bukhamada and Al-Nadhuri were considered.

This, however, appeared on the LNA Twitter account on 11 April:

> All the news about General commander's health are false, Marshal Haftar is in excellent health and he is following his daily general command duties and all op rooms specially Omar Moktar ops room.

As the speculation spread and grew more imaginative, people seemed to have missed the tweet posted on the same day by the head of the United Nations Mission in Libya in which he stated that he had communicated with Haftar by phone and discussed in detail developments in Libya and the political situation.

In the thick of the rumours, many observers were tempted into analysing Haftar's strengths and weaknesses, including me. His talents flourished in Libya at a critical time and probably at no other time and place. First there was his unique ability to cobble together desperate factions into a functioning army. His core support was found in the Sa'adi tribes of East Libya but he had also recruited some Salafist militia which were supported by the Saudi Arabians. Secondly, he had built up and serviced the backing of President Sisi of Egypt and received considerable material support from the UAE, which had established an air bridge via a staging post in Eritrea to keep his forces well equipped. France was supporting him overtly. The French maintained a powerful presence in the Sahel in the shape of roughly 5,000 troops with an HQ in N'Djamena.

Haftar had achieved all this at the age of seventy-four. He had not nominated a successor, probably for fear of a rival but also because there was no one else capable of replacing him. If he died or was medically unfit, the whole show was over. At such a time we may be excused from asking two fundamental questions. Was Libya to be stuck between two choices, the one authoritarian and secular and the other run by Islamist extremists like Islamic State or Ansar al-Sharia? Or was the Tripoli government simply hijacked by the powerful militias in the city?

There was a third question. Was Khalifa Haftar strong enough to rule Libya? Before 2017 he had repeatedly stated that he did not wish to do so, but his statement in December of that year contradicted that. I have drawn attention to only some of those who posed a danger to him in his own back yard, but there were still many more obstacles in the way of a settlement in Libya.

However, Haftar now had to be counted among those who could achieve a solution. His growing importance was illustrated by the spate of ambassadors who visited him: Peter Millet of the UK, Brigitte Curmi of France, Giuseppe Perrone of Italy and Eric Strating of Holland. The UN Special Envoy to Libya, Martin Kobler, also visited him in 2016. It is my view that Haftar was not compromising on his clear and determined claim to gain the command of all Libya's armed forces. But was it an impossible ambition?

8

HAFTAR RETURNS TO LIBYA

Both friends and enemies of Khalifa Haftar had speculated about his health and his possible successors were he to die or retire on health grounds. They awaited his return to Benghazi either in a coffin or as walking wounded.

When Haftar landed at Benina Airport in Libya on 26 April 2018 he was greeted by senior officers of the LNA and notable tribesmen of the region. He gave a short address but failed to speak about his health or explain his recent absence from Libya and public life. Yet he was seated in an elaborate chair while making his speech, giving rise, of course, to further speculation about his ability to continue in command.

Haftar now faced a number of crises. Not the least of these was the nature of the Libyan National Army he commanded. The LNA was now a fragile entity consisting of a typically Libyan group of militias clustered around the 7,000-strong, relatively cohesive core of Haftar's regular army. With the militias, the consensus of opinion was that the LNA could muster around 25,000 men. This is an optimistic figure. If you had simply asked whether Haftar could march into Tripoli at their head, the answer would be no. The militias had their own axes to grind and their loyalty could be strained. It was not unknown for them to clash – in fact, when Haftar's death was erroneously reported, it was painfully clear that his personal command over these disparate groups was the only glue holding them together. The fragile entity over which Haftar presided must have been anxiously awaiting his return.

The question now was, could he rely on them to follow him to Tripoli? He would be unwise to do so. In the battle for Derna, tribal militias had joined Haftar for a number of reasons – including revenge. Some Salafist militias adhered to the LNA but marched to their own music and had been troublesome. How far could Haftar trust them?

Perhaps Haftar had canvassed opinion and reached the conclusion that he and his army would be welcome in Tripoli. But he was still widely perceived as a Ghaddafist and an aspiring strongman. Many in Tripoli thought there was no point in jumping out of the frying pan into the fire.

In this case, the frying pan was the governing force in Tripoli. On 30 March 2016, the Presidential Council of the UN-recognised Libyan Government of National Accord (GNA) had arrived in secret at Tripoli's naval base by boat from Tunisia. It was charged with the government of Libya while preparing for the election of a legislature and government, but there were soon troubles and disagreements. It sat in Tunisia and, fearing violence, was reluctant to move to Tripoli. The Presidential Council was finally pressured by external backers (the UN and Western governments), however, and it relocated to Tripoli even though it did not command any regular forces that could offer it protection. Tripoli by this time was in the thrall of numerous militias which had filled the security gap and become overweening and corrupt. To have consigned the council into the hands of the corrupt militias in Tripoli at such a time was short sighted to say the least.

By the time it arrived in Tripoli, the Presidential Council could only rely on promises of support and protection from a handful of armed groups. A range of other militias were explicitly hostile to it and many other armed groups in Tripoli were on the fence. It transpired that the GNA was unable to bring the militias under control. Worse, they had insinuated themselves into the government administration and were making money corruptly and copiously.

As a result, the GNA – or, to be more accurate, the Presidential Council of the GNA – was deeply implicated in the misuse of funds and unable to function as a government. But as the UN-recognised government it was able to control the Libyan Nation Oil Corporation and to influence the apparently independent Libyan Central Bank. The upshot of this was that the people of East Libya believed that the revenue for 'their oil' was being used improperly. There were no independent auditing arrangements and so the bank was never scrutinised. Of all the issues, this was the most damaging.

In addition, but of no small matter for Haftar, it was implied that the Presidential Council was influenced by the Muslim Brotherhood. This was not appreciated by Egypt and the Gulf States, except Qatar, who supported it along with Turkey. Haftar justified his intention to take his army to Tripoli by saying he would tame the militias, audit the Central Bank and the National Oil Corporation, and remove the Muslim Brotherhood and Islamic extremists.

But to threaten Tripoli, Haftar needed powerful international allies for logistical, financial, diplomatic and military support. He intended, after all, to overthrow the UN-recognised government of Libya. The United Arab Emirates offered essential logistical and operational support and there were signs that it was introducing Chinese drones into service, probably in the battle for Derna. It constructed a large airfield at al-Marj in the Green Mountains to house drones and act as the Libyan end to its air bridge which brought supplies into Libya without troubling the arms embargo patrols in the Mediterranean. Egypt carried out air strikes in Derna and Sirte, particularly in response to the murder by ISIS of twenty-two Egyptian Coptic migrants.

Haftar had stopped off in Cairo on his way home for discussions with President Sisi about the threats posed by Jihadists in Derna and East Libya, and he may have broached the matter of his plans for Tripoli at the time. He had some mopping up to do at home before he could move on, however, and President Sisi was concerned. Haftar's siege of Derna was still active. His forces had thrown a cordon around the city but needed to allow the ordinary citizens medical supplies and sustenance. There were several failures, and tragedies, in this regard and it was a particularly hard nut to crack. The Egyptians were alive to the threat the Derna Islamists posed to their western border and their national security as a whole, and they recognised that Islamist training camps in Derna were preparing terrorists to penetrate Egypt and create instability. No doubt Haftar was able to obtain a guarantee of Egyptian assistance.

President Sisi had more than one reason to fear a militant Islamist regime in East Libya. On 22 July the previous year, he had invited Haftar to join some notable allies of Egypt drawn from the Arab world, with the exception of Qatar, in an inauguration ceremony at a large military base in the Western Desert. Hundreds of tanks, advanced fighter jets, Apache helicopters, Chinook helicopters and armoured vehicles were displayed at the base – touted as the biggest in the Middle East and Africa – in a ceremony designed to impress and deter Egypt's potential enemies. Haftar joined Abu Dhabi's Crown Prince Sheikh Mohammed bin Zayed, Bahrain's Crown Prince Salman bin Hamad Al-Khalifa, Emir of Mecca Prince Khalid Al-Faisal, and Sheikh Mohammad Al-Khalid Al-Hamad Al-Sabah, the Kuwaiti Minister of Defence, at the base 60 kilometres west of Alexandria.

The base was also just a few kilometres from the site of a planned nuclear power plant at al-Dabaa. The plant will have four reactors, the first of which will be operational in 2022, and will eventually supply about 20 per cent of Egypt's power supply. Egypt received a $25 million loan from Russia to meet the cost, and the reactors are to be supplied by the Russian State Nuclear Energy Corporation.

The possibility of an Islamist regime in East Libya would have been sufficient to justify Haftar's presence among the high-powered military guests. His appearance among them will have done him no harm at home and will have signalled that Cairo could not live with ISIS and Ansar al-Sharia so close to its western border. Furthermore, the Egyptians were ready to help Haftar to remove the threats.

There is a second good reason for Haftar's elevation at the ceremony. Egypt needed the base in the Western Desert to protect its massive natural gas discoveries from a belligerent Turkey. In August 2015, an Italian company exploring off the coastal city of Damietta in the southern Mediterranean had stumbled on a significant natural gas field, the Zohr field, which has reserves of 850 billion cubic metres of gas. These substantial natural gas reserves will not only be difficult to exploit for physical reasons, but also because of the pressing difficulties in monetising them. For this to occur, several national interests have to be brought into agreement.

Countries laying claim to a share of the reserves are Greece, Cyprus, Jordan, Lebanon, Egypt and Libya – but not Turkey, as it has no continental shelf falling within the undersea gas fields. The Turks argue that they took a part of eastern Cyprus by force in the 1970s and this gives them access to the gas bonanza, but the claim is only recognised by Turkey itself and antagonises both Cyprus and Greece. But where Turkey does not have access to the Eastern Mediterranean gas reserves, Libya does, giving Turkey an obvious reason for a sudden interest in establishing itself in Libya.

The civil war in Libya provided the perfect opportunity to muscle in, so Turkey tried to pressure Haftar's opponents in Tripoli to sign a treaty which would allow it some leverage. It is as well to remember that Turkey had become heavily dependent on Russian natural gas delivered through the Turk Stream pipeline laid below the Black Sea. It should also be noted that the Turk Stream will, in the near future, be extended to carry Russian natural gas to European countries. The prospect of a confrontation between Egypt and Turkey is thus not impossible. The prospect of a proxy war in Libya, meanwhile, was growing fast.

Haftar's Powerful International Allies

Libya's history has shown us how vulnerable it is to wider regional and international confrontations. We are reminded that it was a part of the Ottoman Empire largely because of its strategic position and the Italian expansion which replaced it. It was fought over in the Second World War and administered by the British until its independence in 1953. Since the Arab Spring, Libya has borne the brunt of proxy confrontations. Haftar's planned attack on Tripoli exacerbated the already aggressive interest of foreign states in Libya, its oil reserves and, wider still, the prospects offered by the Eastern Mediterranean gas fields. Among the other issues provoking international involvement in Libya's civil war were the constant flow, despite the dangers, of the Saharan people traffickers and the haven Libya's Badlands offered to religious extremists and armed rebels bent on overthrowing neighbouring governments.

By April 2019, the regional battle lines were beginning to emerge. While Libya's internal differences were exacerbated by

Haftar's appearance at the gates of Tripoli, the burgeoning proxy war he helped to precipitate began to take over.

The USA, in the hands of President Trump, played a confusing role. Its military presence in the region was found in AFRICOM, based in Stuttgart but with interest in Libya. Haftar has dual US and Libyan citizenship, and when President Trump and Haftar conferred by phone in April 2019, Trump expressed his support for Haftar's drive to take Tripoli. This undermined, at a stroke, the efforts of the British and Italians to raise a UN resolution condemning the use of force in Tripoli, changing the game radically and tipping it in favour of Haftar. However, there was some disagreement between President Trump and the US State Department about Haftar and its lack of resolution left the field open for other actors to take the stage.

For some time, France had been supporting Haftar. It saw the threat of IS and similar Islamic extremists embedded in Libya's lawless south as a threat to the old French Empire states of Chad, Niger, Mali and Burkina Faso. As we have seen, it has a considerable armed presence in the Sahel region, and it is aware that Islamist groups operating in South Libya draw support from allies in Tripoli. Haftar's move to dominate Libya's south-west attracted France's active support. This was made clear in Haftar's propaganda arm (*Address Libya*) on 2 April 2019 in an attempt to justify his attack on Tripoli.

Speaking in an exclusive interview with *Le Figaro*, France's Foreign Minister, Jean-Yves Le Drian, said,

> For a long time, since the French operation Serval 2013 in Mali, we have realized that most weapons came from Libya and that many groups had back bases, starting with AQIM [al-Qaeda]. Remember, al-Qaeda became dominant in Benghazi, US Ambassador Chris Stevens was killed in the same city in 2012, and Daesh [aka ISIS] then infiltrated Libyan territories. . . I had alerted from September

2014, in an interview with *Le Figaro*, on the terrorist risks and on the possibility of local implementation of Daesh. This is exactly what happened: Daesh occupied several Libyan cities and even threatened, at one time, to get its hands on the oil resources.

He went on:

> Since May 2014, LNA, led by Field Marshal Khalifa Haftar, conducted one military operation after another and successfully hunted ISIS and other terrorist groups from one city to the next. LNA first defeated the so-called Shura Council of Benghazi Revolutionaries, a militia alliance which included the group responsible for the attack that killed the U.S. ambassador, after two-month long battle in Benghazi. In October 2014, the terrorist group ISIS took control of numerous government buildings, security vehicles and local landmarks in Derna. LNA launched a military operation in 2015 which successfully liberated the city from ISIS, Al-Qaeda and other extremist groups.
>
> LNA forces and local police began to impose security in previously lawless cities one by one until finally dominating all of Cyrenaica and securing the country's vital oil resources. Earlier this year, LNA mobilized its forces towards the southern region of Fezzan in response to calls made by residents who suffered from the criminal acts of local militias and Chadian armed rebel groups. The residents of Fezzan quickly embraced LNA, which enabled its forces to take control of the region in less than three months.

Two other key players emerged immediately: Turkey and Qatar. Turkey, bordered as it by the Caucasus, the Middle East and the Balkans, has considerable military clout. It is embroiled in the Syrian crisis and in conflict with the Kurds, a people without frontier, and is not unfamiliar with internal security risks. It might be thought that it has enough to do to protect itself. However, the President of Turkey, Recep Tayyip Erdogan, has backed the Muslim Brotherhood and in that stance he is allied to Qatar and finds some sympathy in Tripoli. Qatar, very small but rich in natural gas reserves, is at odds with the other Gulf States and much of the Arab world because it too endorses the Muslim Brotherhood. Turkey has a base in Qatar and supplies military support in return for Qatari money.

While Turkey's military is well equipped and benefits from skilled leadership, military service is compulsory for all male citizens between twenty and forty-one years of age. This limits the use Turkey can make of its own forces and it tends to employ mercenaries in its foreign adventures, of which Libya became one in April 2019. There are added historical ties between Libya and the Ottoman Turks – a mixed blessing in terms of propaganda – and Qatar's involvement in the demise of Muammar Ghaddafi has already been encountered. It is fair to say that Erdogan's Turkey and Qatar began to increase their involvement in Tripoli after Haftar's attack, and the former, attracted by access to the Eastern Mediterranean gas fields, began to send Turkish military advisers to help organise the defence. It also commenced the sale and supply of Turkish Bayraktar drones and Kirpi armoured vehicles. Crucially, Turkey helped Tripoli retake the town of Gharian, which had served as Haftar's forward operating base.

Haftar Returns to Work

As well as international support, to successfully topple Tripoli Haftar would need an army. When he returned to Libya in April 2019, as if from the dead, it is likely that he found the LNA as a regular army of two mechanised infantry brigades, one tank brigade, three artillery brigades, one special forces brigade and two major groupings of smaller units such as light infantry battalions, border guards and security personnel for the oil installations. Haftar's command over these units has at times been challenged, and for good reason. This is Libya, where personality always plays a major role and is often magnified. Ghaddafi, and King Idris before him, was wary of his army officers. Both moved their army commanders around frequently to keep them under the thumb, which was bad for the army if good for personal security.

The nature of the militia groups is also typically Libyan – and often tribal. For example, Haftar's Farjani tribe maintains a militia of around 500 members on which he can depend. The Petroleum Facilities Guard, strongly associated with the al-Magharba tribe, came over to him after its ambitious warlord, Ibrahim Jadhran, was replaced. There are a number of other tribal armed groups in addition, particularly interesting among them being the Awlad Suleiman, which, as we have seen, is highly influential in the south. It was persuaded – with great difficulty – to change its alliance to Haftar.

In West Libya, Haftar claims the support of some of Zintan's powerful militias. These are well-trained, well-supplied and battle-hardened troops. Around 2,500 would probably be available to him were he to be operating in West Libya. This a speculative because the Zintanis, again as we have seen, were divided on the matter of Haftar. A battle for Tripoli would trigger a battle for loyalty in Zintan.

Haftar's air force may have about twenty-seven fighter bombers, seven gunships, fourteen transport helicopters and some transport aircraft, including an IL 76 and a C130. Because of service and maintenance problems it is difficult to assess how many of these assets are operational at any one time. Furthermore, there was another issue of some importance – aircrew training. In some cases, crew may have declined to bomb their own peoples where collateral damage was likely, resulting in the frequent engagement of mercenary aircrews.

There was also some Russian technical support, and Haftar's main base at Benina Airport near Benghazi was enlarged considerably.

Haftar Caught Off Guard?

Haftar's return settled matters for a while but setbacks were inevitable. He was still perceived as vulnerable because of his age and possible health concerns. Moreover, while he had gained control over Libya's oil crescent and seen off the sometime federalist and petty war lord Jadhran, he still needed to win in Derna to establish his claim to lead.

He was soon tested in another arena. Haftar had taken his eye off his western flank and his old enemy Jadhran took advantage. On Thursday 14 June 2018, Jadhran seized the oil terminals at Ras Lanuf and Sidra, attacking both oil ports with the support of the Islamist Benghazi Defence Brigade and an armed group variously described as a Tebu or Chadian rebel militia. Haftar may have reduced his defences around Ras Launf and Sidra in order to stiffen his forces surrounding Derna, where he was taking decisive action against the Islamists who had been dominating the city. Haftar's local commanders there claimed to have liberated more than 75 per cent of the city and expected to drive out the remaining Islamists within days.

There was a fall in Libya's crude oil exports because of Jadhran's attack, and the subsequent damage to the storage capacity at Ras Lanuf was critical. Since the civil war began in 2011, eight of its original thirteen tanks had been destroyed; Jadhran's attack resulted in damage to two more. As Libya's National Oil Corporation pointed out, it would result in the loss of 'hundreds of millions of dollars in construction costs, and billions in lost sales opportunities. Rebuilding the tanks could take years.'

But on 2 June 2018, the Egyptian newspaper *Asharq al-Awsat* reported,

> The Libyan National Army said on Thursday it had rapidly retaken the key oil export terminals of Es Sider and Ras Lanuf, where the head of Libya's National Oil Corporation (NOC) said he hoped operations would resume in a 'couple of days'. Staff were evacuated from the key terminals in Libya's eastern oil crescent and exports were suspended last Thursday when armed groups led by Ibrahim Jathran attacked the ports and occupied them. The closure has led to daily production losses of up to 450,000 barrels per day (bpd), and two oil storage tanks were destroyed or badly damaged by fires during the fighting. For the past week, Khalifa Haftar's LNA has been pounding the area with air strikes as it mobilized to retake the ports, and it continued to target its rivals with air strikes on Thursday as they retreated.

Haftar's Mission Becomes Clearer and He Faces South

By 19 September 2018 there were intimations of Haftar's wider ambitions. Units from the Special Forces of the LNA left the city of Benghazi to commence operations in the south. They were under the command of Major General Wanis Bukhamada, who was tasked with opening an operations room at the Tamanhint Air Force base a short way south-east of Sebha in the Fezzan. Haftar had instructed Bukhamada to 'secure the south of Libya and eliminate terrorist gangs, criminals and mercenaries, and to combat smuggling of arms and drugs and people trafficking'. Bukhamada was and is a formidable fighting soldier who was prominent in the recapture of Benghazi from Islamist militias and the near-complete clearance of Jihadists from Derna. Formidable as he may be, there is no doubt that he has a very tough job to do. To project military power over long distances is not easy, especially in Libya.

Haftar had not signalled his long-term intentions for sending the formidable Bukhamada to pacify the south. Was this move part of a wider plan?

What had Haftar to gain by taking the old province of the Fezzan other than those objectives set out in his instructions to Bukhamada? Two things come to mind. First, he could gain control of the rich oilfields of the Murzuq Basin. In this he would be in competition with the Tripoli government. Second, in dominating the south he threatened Tripoli by shortening the distance between his forward base and the city, thus easing his logistical problems.

Why then had Haftar sent Bukhamada to the south? Since the fall of Ghaddafi in 2011, the south has been largely out of control. He had settled the matter in the south-eastern city of Kufra, some 1020 kilometres from Benghazi and where units associated with the LNA had been for some months under the command of the Kufra Military Zone Commander Brigadier Belgasim Al-Abaj. Brigadier Al-Abaj took up his post there on 16 April 2018. He is a member of the Zawiya tribe, which has dominated the Kufra oasis complex for a long time. Haftar was confident enough in his talents to let Kufra rest in his hands a while, knowing that he dominated the eastern oilfields. It meant he could turn his attention to Bukhamada and the south-west.

Bukhamada's forces were already in control of the Brak al-Shatti and Jufra airbases in southern and central Libya. The Brak al-Shatti military base is in the once-Ghaddafist al-Magraha tribe's homeland. Would Bukhamada succeed in making allies and possessing the famous castle and dominating the fractious city of Sirte and the southern oilfields? It was significant – but somewhat late in the day – that on 5 September 2018 the United Nations representative in Libya, Ghassan Salama, addressed the UN Security Council. He was unhappy about the security situation in Libya. From his words we can get a glimpse of the task Bukhamada faced:

> In recent weeks, Chadian Government and Chadian opposition forces have been fighting, operating from Southern Libya. Over 1,000 fighters have been involved in the hostilities, risking the South becoming a regional battle ground and haven for foreign armed groups, including terrorist organizations. A recent agreement between Chad, Sudan, Niger and Libya needs to be implemented so Libya does not also become an alternative battleground for others. The signatories have asked for support from the International Community for the implementation of these agreements, and I hope that Council members will positively consider their request.

By 24 August Reuters was reporting ominous news:

> Rebels in northern Chad attacked government forces this week at the border with Libya, the fighters and two military sources said on Friday, although the government denied an attack had taken place.

The rebel force appeared to be the Military Command Council for the Salvation of the Republic of Chad (CCMSR), which sought to overthrow President Idriss Déby.

What could the redoubtable Major General Bukhamada and his special forces do to clear the region of IS, al-Qaeda, CCMSR fighters, people traffickers and other malign groups? He could certainly make his peace with the Tebu. The Tebu know, and have recently been in control of, much of South Libya, so recruiting the Tebu militias was among Bukhamada's first tasks. In this, however, he had a troublesome obstacle to overcome in the shape of mercenaries from neighbouring Chad, Niger and the Sudanese province of Darfur, all of whom had their own agenda and were now operating in Libya's south. They had been taking control of the Tebu clans and the municipal councils of the Tebu towns in the Fezzan such as Qaroon, Murzuq, Traagin, and Um Aramyb. They were clearly attracted by the lucrative people-trafficking and smuggling opportunities presented by the open borders.

Bukhamada had been sent into a hornet's nest of tribal and ethnic rivalries. The Arab tribes were making mischief, and thrown into the conflict were the militias attempting to destabilise Chad, thus drawing the French into the mix. There was also some considerable work to do for Bukhamada with the Tuaregs, whose leader, Ali Kanna, appeared to be opposing Bukhamada with the support of the Tripoli-based government.

Obari and Ghat are so-called Tuareg towns and, as we have seen, some Tuaregs also live in Sebha. They were once Ghaddafi's military assets in the Fezzan but they were now much reduced in clout. When Ghaddafi died his Tuareg mercenaries left Libya and, after helping themselves to a considerable quantity of sophisticated weaponry, returned to Mali. There were probably about 100,000 of them, commanded by General Ali Kanna, Ghaddafi's sometime top Tuareg officer. They joined a long-standing rebellion and challenged the Mali government, easily overcoming the local Mali defence system in the northern towns and forming a Tuareg liberation movement. Hitherto the Tuaregs had been a people without a state, and now they described the Tuareg region of Mali as the state of Anzawad. But their ambitions were thwarted by a jihadist group called Ansar Dine which hijacked their rebellion and took control of Mali until they were later ousted by the French.

The resident Tuareg leaders would have to be persuaded not only to remain neutral but to cede the oilfields they guarded to Haftar. Perhaps the Tuareg leadership recognised its own weakness, because in the end they backed Haftar – his people were able to negotiate with the remaining Tuareg around Obari to come over to him, or at least remain passive as he took over

Sebha and the remaining Fezzan cities and the oilfields in the Murzuq Basin. The negotiations must have been interesting and there may be obligations which will weigh Haftar down in the future, but whatever the bargain implied, Haftar's forces took over the Sahara oilfield peacefully. Here is part of Bloomberg's report dated 12 February 2019:

> Forces loyal to Libya's eastern leader Khalifa Haftar have taken control of the country's biggest oil field and say the deposit is secure and ready to resume production.
>
> Haftar's self-styled Libyan National Army fanned out in the southwestern Sharara field, people with knowledge of the matter confirmed. Armed protesters had closed down the 300,000 barrel-per-day deposit in December, demanding more money and investment in the remote region. 'Sharara is completely secure and ready to resume pumping,' LNA spokesman Ahmed al-Mismari said Tuesday in a telephone interview. 'The guards at the field handed over the field to our forces peacefully.'

The LNA had pledged earlier to hand the field over to the National Oil Corporation once it was fully secure. There were a few disputes over the control of the El Fil ('The Elephant') field but the Tariq ibn Ziyad Battalion of the Libyan National Army took it and held it against determined opposition. Tariq ibn Ziyad was a famous military commander who took southern Spain from the Visigoths in the eighth century – Gibraltar is an Anglicization of Jebel Tariq and is named after him. Haftar believed the battalion was as formidable as its name implies.

Haftar's forces then took the cities of Sebha and Murzuq around the middle of March and pushed forward to dominate the towns of Quatrun, Umm Al-Aranib, Ghat and Awaynat. He had done so largely without force of arms but by negotiation, at which he was proving a master. In so doing he placed himself in a dominant position across the main trans-Saharan roads leading from western Chad and eastern Niger to the Mediterranean ports and able to control or eliminate much of the people trafficking, smuggling and legitimate business traffic from the Sahel countries. He had succeeded in dominating nearly 90 per cent of Libya's oil riches and his advance forces were at least 965 kilometres from his main stronghold in Benghazi. What next in the push for Tripoli? The answer was more negotiation.

Haftar's Long Shot

Haftar's mobile forces, together with their commanders, moved via the old trade route from Sebha in the Fezzan to Gharian in the Western Mountains prior to the advance on Tripoli proper. Haftar's forces attacking Tripoli were commanded by Major General Abdul Salam al-Hassi, and by 12 April 2019 it was clear that a large contingent of troops from Bani Walid had arrived to join them.

Haftar's LNA had caught the Government of National Accord's military by surprise by appearing from the south by way of Gharian, the city on the edge of the Western Mountains. This meant his forces had time to bring more reinforcements into play and occupy the southern outskirts of Tripoli before the western militias had time respond. They did so eventually and stalled Haftar's advance, both sides fighting it out through much of April.

But Haftar had miscalculated. Prior to his offensive, politicians and armed groups in West Libya were divided, and he hoped to win many of them over. A handful of armed groups in Tripoli exerted disproportionate influence. They just did not trust each other. Those Tripoli militias which may have supported him failed to rally to his colours.

Italy, who supported the Misratan militias, appeared to be opposing Haftar's attack on Tripoli in diplomatic circles. France, on the other hand, had been supporting Haftar's takeover of

Sebha, and much of the south-east of Libya had thus been placed in a difficult position. Diplomatically, but with tongue in cheek, it urged both sides to stop fighting. Haftar's forces had a number of French military advisers, and the Misratans may have received 'assistance' from Italy. In this context the *Libyan Address* reported this:

> PARIS – The Spokeswoman for the French Foreign Ministry said in an official statement that some groups and persons, classified on the United Nations sanctions list because of their terrorist acts, are involved in the fight in Tripoli against the Libyan National Army (LNA).
>
> The Spokeswoman's comments came in reference to the participation of persons classified internationally on sanctions list the smuggler known as Abdul Rahman al-Miladi, the commander of Al-Somoud Brigade from Misrata Salah Badi, Ibrahim Jidran and other extremists linked to Al-Qaeda such as Ziad Balaam who appeared in the battles within the forces of the Tripoli-based Government of National Accord.

Haftar's allies from the city of Zintan, situated in the Western Mountains, were late in appearing among his coalition of forces on his drive to take Tripoli. The Zintani elders were in favour of joining the attack alongside Haftar but the Minister of Defence, Osama Juwaily, opposed them. He has considerable influence in Zintan, and appeared to have split the city's militias which had so far kept out of the fray. Some experts argued that Haftar had banked on the Zintani militias joining the opening battle on his side and suggest that his advance was fatally flawed as a result. However, by 23 April Major General Idris Madi was leading a large force from Zintan to join Haftar in an attack on Tripoli. It seems that the issues which had detained the formidable Zintanis from joining Haftar had somehow been resolved.

Was Resupply Haftar's Achilles Heel?

Haftar had attacked Tripoli from the south, meaning that supply lines from his base in East Libya were very long. Some observers thought he would run out of fuel and ammunition unless he made a rapid and successful advance to take over his opponent's logistics bases in Tripoli, but it seems his planners found a way to deal with the long distances and unfavourable terrain of his attenuated supply line. The coastal road from Benghazi to Tripoli was controlled by his opponents, the Misratans, from Sirte westwards. This added distance and rough terrain to his problems and, on top of this, in order to outflank his opponents in Misrata, Haftar was forced to route his supply line from the east of Libya though the city of Hun. From road maps of Libya, Hun can be seen to be a critical hub and his opponents spotted this vulnerability and directed air strikes on and around the city. Could Haftar handle the logistical conundrum that bedevilled the British and German armies in the Second World War? His planners had been notable in their success in many ways. Or would logistics be his Achilles heel?

Haftar was soon to find out. On 19 April, his opponents claimed to have pushed his forces out of his forward HQ and logistical base in Gharian in the Western Mountains. If this were true, Haftar's Libyan National Army had a serious resupply problem. He was further troubled when General Ali Kanna, leading a pro-Tripoli 'Southern Protection Force', reappeared and attacked the Tamanhint airbase near Sebha, pressing Haftar's forces to retreat, regroup and return to regain possession of the airbase. Tripoli was endeavouring to harass Haftar.

Putin Tries to Mediate

Turkey too had become belligerent. On 3 January 2020, the Turkish parliament voted to send troops at the request of the Libyan Government of National Accord (GNA) whose militias were under attack on the outskirts of Tripoli by the LNA. Some Turkish units had already been positioned in Tripoli and had, so far, opened an operations room from which they were helping the GNA's attempts to defend itself from Haftar's forces. Turkish drones were already being used in the defence of Tripoli and were operated by Turkish 'pilots'.

Turkey had been roundly condemned for this aggressive move by Egypt, Algeria and the African Union. Algeria stated that it would not stand by and allow Turkish interference in Libya and Tunisia stated that it would not offer Turkey bases from which to launch attacks. The African Union was anxious about the effect of its interference in Libya on the Sahel states, which were not stable. Turkey had already severely antagonised Greece and Cyprus by its dispute of the sovereignty of some of the Greek islands and its invasion of Cyprus in the 1970s.

Then there were the reports that Syrian militias were being offered Turkish citizenship and big money to fight in Libya. Elizabeth Tsurkov, a Research Fellow at the US-based Foreign Policy Research Institute, stated that 'sources inside the Turkish-backed Syrian factions tell me that in exchange for fighting in Libya, fighters are being promised Turkish citizenship after 6 months of deployment'. Much of the armaments, including drones, which Turkey has sent to aid the GNA have been shipped into Libya via Misrata's port. The Misrata 'Flying School' has been used as a base for the GNA's air force.

Haftar, from his headquarters in Benghazi, reacted decisively to the Turkish threat. His forces held sway over East Libya, including the so-called oil crescent around the Gulf of Sirte and in the Fezzan. On Monday 6 January, units of his LNA marched into Sirte virtually unopposed. The GNA's militias hitherto in possession of the city retreated towards Misrata. Now Haftar's forces announced the expansion of the warzone near Misrata and declared a no-fly zone which extended over Tripoli. The no-fly zone came into effect at 21.00 local time on 9 January and included Tripoli's Mitiga airport. Civil airlines were warned that their aircraft risked destruction if they attempted to ignore the no-fly zone.

But this was Haftar's Plan B. He had failed in his Plan A when the expected rally to his side failed to emerge when his son arrived at the gates of Tripoli on that fateful day. Now his strategy was to encircle the capital and Misrata, make gradual fighting inroads into Tripoli and squeeze them into submission. However, the Misrata militias were battle hardened and aggressive and Haftar may have hoped that the Turks would be discouraged from committing a large expeditionary force in Libya by international condemnation. Much would depend on the attitude adopted by the Misrata militias in the face of a potential large-scale Turkish intervention.

To rachet up the pressure, Haftar now called for a 'jihad' against the Turks and there was lingering resentment among many in Libya about Turkey's long sojourn among their ancestors. Turkey had recently signed a treaty with the GNA in Libya which allowed it some leverage in Libya's claim to part of the Eastern Mediterranean gas reserves. This was antagonising the legitimate claimants considerably.

In response to Turkey's proposed military support for the Tripoli GNA, Algeria made it clear that it would not happily tolerate foreign intervention in Libya and the African Union was clearly opposed to Turkey's belligerent threats. Italy, at one time a potential ally of Turkey against Haftar, was somewhat restrained by indecision. It was clear that Turkey's belligerence when it proclaimed its intention to send troops to aid Haftar's enemies caused consternation, and now Egypt was preparing to demonstrate its opposition with naval exercises in or near Libya's territorial waters.

Internationally, Haftar had been successful in gaining support. He had the backing of, among others, Egypt, France, the UAE and Russia, plus the tacit support of his southern neighbours such as Chad and Niger. At one time President Trump had also voiced his backing, but his somewhat bellicose remarks were modified by more balanced and statesmanlike communiques later. Nevertheless, the USA was seriously concerned about the presence of IS and al-Qaeda in Libya and it is likely that they had enthusiastic allies in some of the militias supporting the GNA.

Haftar had been recruiting Sudanese militias from Darfur. This showed that he was finding it difficult to recruit and train sufficient Libyan troops to keep control of his widely dispersed territory and its diverse population while at the same time maintaining long and vulnerable supply lines. The long and costly urban battle he would doubtless face were he to continue his advance on Misrata and Tripoli might be a battle too far. His fight to expel radical Islamist militias from Benghazi and Derna had been prolonged and dirty, and both places lack the glamour and public scrutiny of Tripoli. In public relations and propaganda terms he may have calculated that the vicious and costly nature of urban warfare would arouse so much anti-Haftar sentiment in the capital city that it would be counterproductive.

He may also have been sufficiently self-aware to know that there were traits in his personality and incidents in his history which made him potentially unpopular. His dual Libyan-US citizenship still does not sit well with some factions in Libya, and his notable ability to raise an army and wield it well may not transfer into political successes.

Enter Putin. The Russian president, ever the opportunist, was in frequent telephone communication with Erdogan, especially during the events around the opening of the Turk-Stream pipeline supplying Russian natural gas to Turkey. The influence he secured was enough to give pause to Turkey's belligerence and persuade Haftar to travel to Moscow and potentially sign a peace treaty with the GNA. Haftar agreed to go. Why, after all this time, did he feel that the time was ripe to bring the fighting to an end and commence negotiations leading to a possible settlement in Libya?

Haftar would not have agreed to go to Moscow as a supplicant. His forces had recently taken the strategically important city of Sirte and he had been strong enough to declare a no-fly zone over Tripoli. He may have reasoned that, while he held some good cards, he had reached a point where the risk inherent in further military action was too great. In other words, he may have calculated that taking Misrata and Tripoli would be costly – both militarily, politically and internationally.

9

END GAME?

Despite the profound and daunting disruption caused by the Covid-19 pandemic, as 2020 drew to a close, the balance of power in Libya could be changed – by Recep Tayyip Erdogan. In January, when Erdogan and Putin invited Haftar to Moscow to broker a peace deal with the GNA, the weakness in Haftar's defences was easy to see. The interesting question was, could Erdogan exploit it?

Erdogan has long pursued a high-risk policy at home in Turkey and engaged in some dangerous foreign adventures. He has survived a coup and reacted to it with a heavy hand. He has taken risks with his relationships with the EU and the US which may cause him grief if the Turkish economy fails. He has courted Putin, who is a dangerous ally and a ruthless enemy, sometimes simultaneously. He has antagonised his near neighbours in the Eastern Mediterranean. He has also banked heavily on his alliance with Qatar, which puts him at odds with the other Gulf States, and his dealings with Iran are tricky. His is a high-wire act and there are some who anticipate his fall.

But as we have seen, Turkey has considerable military clout. To put its military power in perspective, there are around 570,000 regulars and 429,000 reservists on its nominal roll and it is the second-largest force in NATO, being equal in size to the combined forces of Britain and France. Turkey has a base in Qatar, where it supplies military support in return for Qatari money. The Qatari alliances are interesting. For example, at the end of 2017 Qatar agreed to buy twenty-four Typhoon jets from Britain's BAE Systems in a deal worth around £5 billion. This must cramp the style of British diplomats in dealing with Qatar. The contract also includes the supply of nine Hawk T2 aircraft, and the RAF's No. 12 Squadron began integrating Qatari personnel, including pilots and groundcrew, in 2019. The personnel are for the time being stationed at RAF Coningsby but will later move to Qatar. The joint squadron aims to have the Qatar Emiri Air Force prepared for the arrival of the first QEAF Typhoon in 2022.[15]

But Turkish military efficiency has suffered several blows, not least the arrest of a number of military personnel, among whom were up to a third of Turkey's senior commanders, following a failed coup against Erdogan in 2016. Reports of mistreatment are not unusual.

But in January 2020, Turkey had the GNA over a barrel. Since late 2018, Turkey had been asking the Tripoli Government of National Accord (GNA) to sign a memorandum of understanding that would allow it access to the gas reserves in the Mediterranean. The GNA had long been reluctant to sign the deal. Now, the GNA was desperate for Turkish military support and arms – Haftar was getting closer by the hour to the symbolic heart of Tripoli, the great square in the shadow of the Red Castle.

There was more, however, than a hydrocarbon bonanza propelling Erdogan's thrust into Libyan affairs. Soner Cagapty, the Beyer Family Fellow and Director of the Turkish Research Program at the Washington Institute, suggests that there is a new dynamic in Turkey labelled by some as 'Ottomanism'. Cagapty

15. https://www.forces.net/news/uk-qatar-joint-typhoon-squadron-marked-ceremony

examines the hypothesis that there is a growing interest among influential Turks in forging relationships with Muslim-majority countries rather than focusing on Western nations. In particular, some thinkers in Turkey who are said to be in Erdogan's orbit are embracing Ottomanism. Among them are some for whom Islam is the core of Turkish identity, and they go as far as to assume the right and the duty to defend Muslims in the former Ottoman Empire.

It is not unusual to read that some Turkish influencers are harking back to the breakup of the old Ottoman Empire after the First World War and portraying the new frontiers drawn on the maps at the time as colonialist impositions which caused artificial redistribution of the old empire to Christian imperialist beneficiaries, the British in particular. It is still possible to raise the spectre of Perfidious Albion. Certainly, Erdogan was and is making every effort to re-establish links with Muslim countries once in the Ottoman Empire – and that includes Libya.

Libya and the Ottomans

The Ottoman Turks have a long relationship with Libya, and Erdogan is an authoritarian leader who is not averse to rewriting history if it helps. He has been known to overlook the bad bits. The Knights Hospitallers occupied Tripoli in the sixteenth century in order to defend the sea lanes to the south of their stronghold in Malta. Their tenure was insecure, and they were summarily ejected by the corsair Dragut (aka Turgut Rais) and a number of followers in August 1551.

Heroes help warmongers, and Dragut, much admired now in Turkey, was made an admiral in the Ottoman navy. He was born in Anatolia to Greek parents and went to sea at the age of twelve. A talented soldier and sailor, he rose to become a protégé of Hayrettin, one of the famous Barbarossa brothers. He was a corsair, a privateer operating with a letter of marque from the

Ottoman sultan. Like Oruch Barbarossa, he too was captured and enslaved by Christians, an experience which strengthened his commitment to piracy in the name of Islam. After he captured Tripoli from the Knights Hospitallers, the ambitious and ruthless Dragut was appointed Sanjak Bey of the province of Tripolitania.

Dragut and his fellow corsairs were unable to hold Tripoli with their limited resources, so they ceded it to the Sultan of Turkey and it was absorbed into the Ottoman Empire. The Ottomans extended their rule southwards from Tripoli so that, by 1580, they had finally made allies of the chiefs of the Fezzan, thus securing the trans-Saharan slave trade for the Tripoli merchants. Tripoli was to remain, though sometimes only nominally, a Turkish province for the next three hundred years. The slave trade was to continue until 1911.

Dragut was killed on 23 June 1565 in the great battle between the Ottomans and the Hospitallers of St John in Malta. His body was shipped to Tripoli and buried in the Dragut Mosque behind the Red Castle. The mosque is still in use today. It is this sort of history that Erdogan repackages. Dragut's statue in Istanbul is cast in heroic bronze with a hand resting on a globe.

But how easily we forget our history. Today it would be possible for someone to attend the Dragut Mosque and then see Turkish warships offshore and Turkish merchant vessels in the harbour unloading military hardware in defiance of the Libyan arms embargo. Turkish sea power has re-emerged – the Turks are back.

Erdogan and Putin

We can speculate about Erdogan and Putin's aims in inviting Haftar to Moscow in January 2020, but they were unlikely to be entirely altruistic. Putin and Erdogan had previously been successful in arranging local peace treaties in Syria and were frequently in communication. Erdogan was developing an active and sometimes adversarial foreign policy, which had manifested itself in Libya, and Putin was also interested in Haftar. Haftar was, no doubt, alive to all of this but went to Moscow anyway and listened to their proposals.

Russian and Turkish sources offer us a different narrative of the outcome. Erdogan tells us that Field Marshal Haftar lurked in his hotel room throughout the proceedings and was but an upstart war lord. Russian sources say that Haftar took two days to decide how to respond to the draft agreement that they had already hammered out and had signed by Fayez al-Serraj for the GNA.

The Russians suggest that Haftar consulted with the tribes, which supported him while weighing his decision. In the light of subsequent events this may be true. What is clear is that Haftar declined to sign the peace treaty and left Moscow abruptly, arguing that the deal did not allow for a satisfactory timetable for disbanding the Tripoli militias.

Erdogan was furious. But although Haftar had certainly gambled, at least he was consistent. He had long held, and expressed, the view that the Tripoli militias were corrupt and contained too many militant Islamists. It has been one of his principal aims to defeat them and establish an independent police force and judiciary. He would not abandon one of his key objectives and put his long-planned and, so far, carefully executed Plan B in peril. He may have been gambling on having the strength and outside support to win the battle for Tripoli.

Haftar's international support was certainly impressive. France backed him, seeing the threat of IS and similar Islamic extremists as threats to the old French Empire states of Chad, Niger, Mali and Burkina Faso. Haftar had their support in both military hardware and the equally powerful field of propaganda. France, it is easy to forget, is a Mediterranean power with large Muslim communities. Its colonial past is more to be found in the photograph albums of grandparents but it needs both the yellow cake uranium from Niger and control of the flow of migrants from its old empire. Its interest in Libya is defensive and it has often deployed its soft power in aid of Haftar. Perhaps 'soft power' has become a misnomer.

In an interview with France's Foreign Minister, Jean-Yves Le Drian, in an April 2019 edition of *Le Figaro*, the language of propaganda is easy to spot. Haftar is portrayed as taming 'the previous lawless cities one by one' and 'mobilizing' the LNA towards the Fezzan in response to residents who 'suffered from criminal acts' of local militias. It is easy to nod as the phrases march past like well-drilled guardsmen. The strong man is taking the salute; all is well. It fits nicely with the tag line from the LNA Facebook's 'About' page:

> No to the Brotherhood, no to Da'aish, yes to the Libyan Army and its leader Marshall Khalifa Haftar, may God protect him.

Le Drian also hints at Haftar's strategy, describing the Libyan as having concentrated on taking the main population centres – that is Benghazi, Derna, Ajdabiya, Sebha and Sirte – one at a time. He brought the major tribes on side to give him territorial reach and control over the sources of oil and its means of export. He aimed to take Tripoli by a combination of threat and guile and when that failed surrounded the Tripoli oasis with his forces and commenced the slow process of taking the city by increments and ultimately by controlling its main source of income.

The Ceasefire

Erdogan and Putin must have been aware that just days after the meeting in Moscow, on 19 January 2020, the international effort to bring peace to Libya would focus on a conference in Berlin attended by German Chancellor Angela Merkel, British Prime

Minister Boris Johnson, and French President Emanuel Macron as well as heads of state, ministers and diplomats from Italy, Turkey, the USA and Russia among others. Field Marshal Khalifa Haftar and the head of the GNA, of course, also attended. Like Erdogan and Putin's attempt in Moscow, the primary purpose of the conference was to establish an agreement between the GNA and Haftar, or at least the means of achieving one. But like Erdogan and Putin, it seems that some of those striving for a settlement were busy disturbing the peace themselves.

While the conference proceeded, world attention was drawn to some corroborated reports from Egyptian and Libyan sources that the eastern oil ports had been closed by tribes in support of Haftar. The tribes were said to be opposing the arrival of Turkish-sponsored mercenaries from Syria to strengthen the GNA. Does this explain why Haftar consulted the tribes during his two days of deliberations in Moscow? Of course, Haftar's LNA held East Libya and thus the important oilfields and the oil ports around the Gulf of Sirte and the oil port near the eastern city of Tobruk. But what about the Murzuq oilfields?

Within a short time, it was reported that tribes in Libya's south-west had also occupied the Murzuq oil fields, thus closing down the whole of Libya's oil industry. Haftar had shown the length of his arm and had implemented his Plan B with impeccable timing. Libya's oil revenue is paid to the Tripoli-based Libyan National Oil Company, which had hitherto remained relatively neutral despite the schisms caused by the long years of armed strife in Libya. Haftar had taken physical control of the oilfields but was powerless to sell the oil. Nevertheless, he had achieved what he set out to do; the gesture was not intended for profit but to squeeze the GNA.

Turkey's belligerent attempt to send troops – or at least Turkish-sponsored militias – to the assistance of Haftar's enemies clearly had the effect of uniting powerful Libyan tribes against what they perceived as an attempt to revive Ottoman rule in Libya. The tribes likely to be involved in the closure of the oil ports were among those same tribes which cooperated with the Libyan resistance hero Omar al-Mukhtar in the long rebellion against the Italian occupation of Libya which followed the removal of the Turks in 1911. These tribes would be profoundly opposed to the perceived attempt by Turkey to renew Ottoman-like ambitions.

But there was a deeper reason for their opposition: a grievance among the tribes about the revenue from the oil harvested from beneath their land being used to pay the Turkish-sponsored militias. These are the tribes in whose homeland the eastern oil ports are found – the al-Magharba, which houses the Ras Lanuf, Marsa Brega and al-Zuetina terminals, and the al-Obaidat, which is home to the Tobruk oil terminal. The Zawia tribe (known locally as the Sway) holds control over the oilfields and much of the pipelines.

To the surprise of many onlookers, the Libyan National Oil Company stated,

> The blockade instructions were given by Maj Gen Nagi al-Maghrabi, the commander of Petroleum Facilities Group (Sic) appointed by the Libyan National Army, and Col Ali al-Jilani from the LNA's Greater Sirte Operations Room.

Major General Nagi al-Maghrabi's tribal affiliations are clear: the Petroleum Facilities Guard is a paramilitary force which guards the Libyan oil assets such as the oil ports around the Gulf of Sirte known as the 'Oil Crescent'. The oil ports can only have been taken over by those who were paid to guard them.

Despite the best efforts of those around the conference tables, the battle for Tripoli continued. The report made by the United Nations Mission to Libya in February 2020 stated,

The intensity of the attacks in Libya's west became acute during the political and military talks. . . On 18 February, the Libyan National Army targeted the Tripoli port with a barrage of heavy artillery and Grad rockets aimed at destroying a cargo vessel allegedly delivering military equipment to the Government of National Accord.

Later that day and on 29 February, un-crewed aerial vehicles operated in support of the Government of National Accord attempted to target Libyan National Army positions south of the Ayn Zarah district, but were shot down by Libyan National Army air defence systems. The concentration of forces by both parties was confirmed in the Zatarnah area and Qarabulli, where clashes had been reported, with the Libyan National Army unsuccessfully attempting to reach the eastern coastal road to disrupt the connection between Misratah and Tripoli. In addition, major Libyan National Army reinforcements reportedly arrived in Aziziyah and the Hayrah area north of Gharian, which the Libyan National Army lost to the Government of National Accord in June 2019 and has been trying to reclaim. On 22 January, the Libyan National Army further extended its previously declared no-fly zone southwards, towards Gharian and Tarhuna, and threatened to shoot down any military or civilian aircraft approaching Mitiga Airport, in Tripoli. The airport was targeted in a string of Libyan National Army attacks with indirect fire by forces, with a peak of 50 shells on 28 February. The attacks disrupted the airport's operation and resulted in civilian casualties and damage to nearby civilian homes.[16]

There were more peace conferences to come, but they too met with failure. Haftar's Plan B, which by now there was sufficient

---

16. https://unsmil.unmissions.org/sites/default/files/s_2020_360_e. pdf

evidence to discern, might explain why. But only those in Haftar's inner circle would have any real knowledge of it.

Yet, if we survey Haftar's assets and liabilities as he left the Kremlin – and an angry Erdogan – in January 2020, might we see a fatal flaw? He had thrown a cordon around the Tripoli oasis, taken control over all Libya's oil facilities and, like T. E. Lawrence in another theatre of war, corralled an impressive list of international allies. He could afford the best mercenaries, call on drones and make modern, mind-bending propaganda. Yet with all of that he decided to risk it, to rachet up the pressure and grind his way into Tripoli's soft centre. Had he one more ace to play as he arrived at his HQ?

Turkey had seen a weakness in Haftar's position and was ready to test his strength and that of his international support. On the other side, Russia had seen an opportunity for a low-cost, high-yield intervention. They both staked a claim in Libya, and Haftar made a fatal miscalculation. He was overextended by a long way and his supply lines were easy targets. When he implemented his oilfield shutdown he had been just strong enough to strike a peace deal. The French no doubt told him to make the best of it and cut a deal before it slipped from his grasp.

Erdogan was by now determined to raise the stakes and win. His motives have been discussed and there is no doubt that he was ready to be ruthless. He decided to increase his naval assets. This would have two major effects – it would allow him to ignore the arms embargo and would also enable him to ship more equipment and Syrian mercenaries into Tripoli under the protection of his warships. He was defiant enough to take the flack.

In response, on 17 February 2020, a concerned European Union launched a naval blockade of the Mediterranean, codenamed Operation Irini, in an effort to enforce the UN arms embargo on Libya. The Italian, French, Greek and German navies all contributed vessels, aircraft and drones to the operation. The GNA in Tripoli and Turkey complained loudly but continued to ignore it. They had one good argument: Haftar was being supplied by air by the UAE and by land from the east. One violation was as good as another.

A Blow to Haftar

Meanwhile, the body count was mounting. A report by the United Nations Support Mission in Libya (UNSMIL) carried this report in full in the *Libya Herald* on 12 May 2020:

> Following a relative reduction in fighting in the immediate aftermath of the truce of 12 January called for by the Presidents of the Russian Federation and Turkey and accepted by the Government of National Accord and the Libyan National Army, fighting gradually resumed. Both parties redeployed forces along the front lines in the Tripoli area. As at 21 April, more than 850 reported breaches of the ceasefire had been recorded by UNSMIL, including an unprecedented increase in indirect fire observed in urban areas, resulting in civilian casualties, damage to civilian infrastructure and disruption of commercial air operations. At other flashpoints in western Libya, tensions also remained high. On 26 January, the Libyan National Army launched an offensive against the forces of the Government of National Accord in the Abu Qurayn area, south of Misratah, prompting heavy clashes and casualties on both sides. At the end of March, heavy artillery fire and rocket attacks were continued by both sides in parts of southern Tripoli and in the central and western regions. Locations along the western coastal road towards the border with Tunisia were seized by the forces of the Government of National Accord in mid-April. On 18 April, those forces launched a coordinated attack against the city of Tarhunah.

Reports continued of foreign mercenaries providing the Government of National Accord and the Libyan National Army with enhanced combat capabilities, amid persistent reports of military equipment and arms being supplied to both sides in violation of the United Nations-imposed arms embargo. Those developments undermined United Nations-led dialogue initiatives and added to more human suffering. From 1 January to 31 March, there were at least 131 civilian casualties in Libya, including at least 64 persons who were killed. Since April 2019, more than 200,000 persons have been forced to leave their homes in and around Tripoli owing to armed conflict.[17]

The GNA launched Operation Peace Storm, which it said was a response to the increased attacks by the LNA on civilian neighbourhoods in Tripoli. The military escalation complicated efforts by civilian authorities and the population towards putting preventive measures in place to address the Covid-19 pandemic.

By now, Erdogan's frigates gave him a number of weapons platforms within range of Haftar's forces, provided command and control for his drones and, crucially, were helping to immobilise Haftar's anti-aircraft defences. The Turkish strongman was ready to deploy his drones and anti-aircraft assets and use them imaginatively. Though his drones were medium range and needed local command and control, unlike the UAE's Wing Loongs, they were homemade and he could experiment with them to improve their performance and that of their operators.

The conduct of the Turkish support for the GNA could well be included in staff training by a number of countries in the future because it demonstrates the Turkish talent for frugal, resourceful

---

17. https://www.libyaherald.com/2020/05/12/report-of-the-un-secretary-general-antonio-guterres-on-libya-to-the-security-council/

and imaginative planning. They are good soldiers. They did well at Gallipoli, and in Libya they have been creative, especially in the use of their homemade tactical drone, the Bayraktar TB2. It has a range of more than 150 kilometres and can fly at a maximum altitude of 22,500 feet. With a maximum speed of 70 knots and endurance of more than twenty hours, it is the brainchild of Selçuk Byraktar, an MIT alumnus and enterprising engineer who married President Erdogan's daughter. It is in service within Turkey, and has been exploited tactically with notable success in Syria. By the time it reached Libya its production costs had reduced and its handlers had learned a lot about how to use it tactically. Turkey could afford to sacrifice a few to learn how to knock out the Russian anti-aircraft weapons in Haftar's armoury.

In March 2020, Turkey launched dozens of drone strikes in Syria as part of a combined air and ground operation. Turkey's drones targeted armoured vehicles, air-defence systems, and opposition personnel. Drones make soldiers nervous. It must indeed be disconcerting that the operator intent on killing you is sitting in a comfortable chair in a distant control room; this, of course, is one of the principal reasons they are effective. The Syrian Civil War widened the TB2's potential on the battlefield, and the lessons learned here were passed on and improved upon in Libya. Nowadays, skilled pilots who fly combat aircraft are expensive and rare, and Haftar's main backers, the UAE and France, were reluctant to commit their pilots too often for fear of one being shot down only to appear on social media being tortured.

Initially, the drones were successful in disrupting Haftar's supply lines and killing his senior officers. The air cover they provided also allowed the GNA to recapture a series of towns north-west of Tripoli. In the days leading up to 18 May 2020, Turkish drones systematically silenced the Russian made anti-aircraft defences at the al-Watiya airfield some 90 miles south-west of Tripoli. This was a technical feat of no mean proportions. It put Haftar's forces on the back foot and opened the base, which was also Haftar's forward command HQ and logistics hub, to increasing attacks by drones. He was seriously overextended and his road-based supply lines were now also vulnerable to Turkish drones. Without al-Watiya, his vital air bridge was also out of action. He would be beaten. The speed at which the Russian Wagner mercenaries escaped from there to a sanctuary in the east will bear further research.[18]

Once the GNA forces had captured al-Watiya, Haftar was in retreat. He was unable to match the combination of experienced Syrian militias imported by Turkey into Tripoli and the well-handled drones seeking out his forces and strafing them. The Turkish drones gave the battle-hardened Syrian mercenaries navigation, intelligence and artillery cover and thus a considerable, probably critical, edge.

The Turks had brought more than 15,000 Syrians into Libya and had equipped them well. The question of who was paying for them hung over the public debate and helped Haftar's propagandists, who pointed out that Libyan oil was footing the bill. Haftar put a good face on it, but they forced him to retreat and lose morale and ground fast. His ground forces were targeted by drones as they retired over open country and he was forced to stand on a line drawn from the west of Sirte to his air base at Jufra.

His international allies were also forced to adjust. Haftar's Russian Wagner mercenaries lost face and retreated behind his new defensive lines. Turkey's intervention had made the difference and Haftar's allies were not amused. France began to condemn

18. https://www.theguardian.com/world/2020/may/18/forces-allied-to-libyan-government-retake-key-al-watiya-airbase

Turkey again for its flagrant violations of the Libyan arms embargo.

Alarmed, President Sisi of Egypt decided to act. He made it known that Haftar's new defensive position was a red line for him. He stated that if the GNA and Erdogan's Syrians crossed it, Egypt would respond in force. In effect, he pitched Egypt against Turkey.

On 4 July, Haftar's Emirati supporters sent Turkey a warning in kind. Al-Watiya base was attacked from the air without warning. No one has yet claimed responsibility for the raid but the planning and execution made it a near-certainty that France or the UAE were the perpetrators and Dassault Mirage 2000-9s or Rafale F3-R the likely aircraft involved – though that is a hypothesis based only on extensive press coverage.

The aircraft were apparently routed from the Egyptian base near Mursa Matruh on a south-westerly track to avoid the Turkish radar and then turned north to al-Watiya. They were able to breach the anti-aircraft defences on the night of 4 July in a series of nine attacks and do lasting damage with an accuracy that indicates highly skilled pilots.

The raid was not intended to retake al-Watiya but to warn the Turks that they should not try to attack Haftar's new defences behind the line just west of Sirte to the Jufra air base. There were three other possible motives, too. One was to destroy the two MIM-23 Hawk anti-aircraft batteries just installed by the Turks. Haftar's rapid retreat in the face of superior arms augmented by Syrian militias had caused him to lose face – a matter of significance in Arab countries in particular. There was, and still is, the damning case of human rights violations which came to light when the GNA occupied the city of Tarhuna in the wake of Haftar's retreat. Tarhuna was a small town still favoured by Italian farmers when I was stationed nearby at Tripoli's international airport in the 1950s. The British Royal

Air Force maintained a bombing range in the vicinity and employed members of the Tarhuna tribe. The town now calls itself a city and it is here that on 5 June 2020 advance parties of GNA fighters found piles of bodies stacked up in the local hospital morgue. They later found fresh mass graves. It will take a long time to deal with this number of bodies and more are still being found according to social media. They mention figures of 300 and counting. Is this a war crime or a civil crime of unusual severity? If it is the former, Khalifa Haftar must answer in the court of public opinion, even if he was not directly responsible. The Kani militia of Tarhuna, which has been discussed already, allied itself with Haftar when his advance patrols arrived in Tripoli's suburbs. It had not been expected to do so but Haftar must have agreed to the alliance in the hope that Tripoli would fall quickly and he could handle problems arising at his leisure. He, or his staff, cannot have been unaware that the seven Kani brothers who 'owned' the militia were making money by dubious means and ruling Tarhuna aggressively. For Haftar it was a marriage of convenience which he may come to regret. He has been implicated in crimes against humanity in Chad and Benghazi, but this one is much more severe and at the same time difficult to judge. Either way, some distraction was necessary and the audacious raid on al-Watiya provided it. It could not do so for long, however.

Those who become professional soldiers, sailors or airmen must do so with the knowledge that they may have to kill or order someone to kill. They expect to do so in accordance with the law and at the behest of politicians in lawful government and under their protection. Problems arise when they have to kill in times of civil unrest or become involved in actions on behalf of foreign powers. Actions by special forces are interesting in this regard. The issue is fraught and there are outstanding matters arising around it in Northern Ireland and in Kenya, for example. There is evidence of what is now termed 'moral injury' suffered by military personnel who are required to carry out acts against their moral code. In a civil war the matter becomes even more complicated, and especially so when local militias are involved. In the case of the Kani militia, more complications come into play. It is beginning to appear that the Kani family became more paranoid and more violent with time and that some of the killings they committed in Tarhuna were personal. The status in law of the Kani militia when the killings took place needs some thought, as the issue may be criminal and not attributable to Haftar. Nevertheless, his moral standing may be challenged. As the French thinker Grégoire Chamayou has written, the category of 'combatant' (a legitimate target) has already tended to 'be diluted in such a way as to extend to any form of membership of, collaboration with, or presumed sympathy for some militant organization'.[19]

By now proper persons should have been appointed to investigate events in Tarhuna, but it looks as though it will be a long time before there is some resolution. Specialists are now working in the killing fields. At best, Haftar became a hostage to fortune the moment he embarked upon dealings with the Kani brothers.

Haftar's story was being transformed because modern warfare has changed radically. Sometimes in history you see a weapon that shifts warfare to a new level. Greek fire did it, as did the longbow and the rifle. The weaponizing of propaganda has been virulent and is growing even more infectious, if that is possible. But the drone is a game-changing weapon on a level with the tank at the end of the First World War. Haftar now had plenty of them, thanks to the UAE, and Tripoli had even more thanks to Turkey. But how do they measure up against each other?

---

19. https://www.theguardian.com/news/2020/oct/15/dangerous-
    rise-of-military-ai-drone-swarm-autonomous-weapons

China's Pterodactyls, Putin's Chef and Wagner's Ring

Over half a century ago I would drive the long road to Tobruk and sometimes visit its nearby Royal Air Force station at El Adem. Back then it was a remote and lonely place to be, but in recent times it has gained some new occupants in the shape of the UAE personnel looking after and flying a fleet of Chinese drones on behalf of Haftar's LNA. The Wing Loong (Pterodactyl) had been in service with Haftar since 2016, and it had proved useful in his long but successful siege of Derna. It is cheap by comparison to American drones, and the Chinese will sell to anyone with the money to buy. The Wing Loong has a combat radius of 1,500 kilometres so it can deliver precision-guided ordinance and gather intelligence anywhere in Libya. Haftar's forces made good use of it in Tripoli but there was some collateral damage, and it does have its limitations. One is that, because it is bought off the shelf, there is no way for the user to adapt the design to suit the task.

There is a contrast between these highly sophisticated drones and the forces on the ground in Libya. It is not entirely in jest that some say a war lord can arm a large group of young men with AK47s, a pair of boots and a supply of weed and launch them against soft targets with devastating effect. As the Toyota Wars in Chad showed, in the confrontation between Ghaddafi's lavishly equipped army and his Chadian vanquishers in their pickup trucks, the latter were able to benefit from sophisticated intelligence-gathering techniques and lightweight, easy-to-use modern weaponry using guile and speed. The nature of the conflict had changed and the Libyans did not adapt. They were fighting an old war.

Arab armies, the LNA among them, are often accused of inadequate training. The Libyan *thuwwars* in 2011 were criticised for retreating too rapidly. That was not true in Misrata and Haftar's LNA fought tenaciously in the Fish Market battles in

Benghazi. The real problem is in the words we use. Instead of asking if the Tripoli and LNA militias were adequately trained, we should ask if they were *appropriately* trained. Up to this point they were appropriately trained, but circumstances had changed radically. A new breed of mercenary had been hired by Haftar.

In March 2019, reports were circulating that a large number of mercenary snipers belonging to the Russian Wagner Group, a private military contractor, were operating with the LNA. There are a good number of PMCs available for hire, some of which are British, but the Wagner PMC is said to be closely connected to the Russian military, some say very closely. It is apparently owned by a Russian entrepreneur who also owns a catering company which does business with the Kremlin. He is jokingly referred to as Putin's chef. The group is named after the call sign of its founding mercenary, who has a taste for Wagner's *Ring*.

A Standoff and Some Friction in Tripoli

On 20 August, a ceasefire was declared between the Tripoli and pro-Haftar forces facing off at the Sirte-Jufra line which was still threatened despite President Sisi's stated intention to intervene if it was attacked. Haftar embarked on a combined campaign of consolidation and propaganda from his HQ. He summoned his senior commanders to a conference during which he alerted them to the strong possibility that the GNA and Erdogan would attack and try to take the oil crescent, and tasked them with its defence. He was seen promoting his senior officers in recognition of their good service and he made statements positioning his army as the one stable body in Libya.

He then appeared to step back and let the politicians take the lead. Was he still waiting for the people to call for his leadership or did he detect a profound weariness among Libyans and a lack of enthusiasm for more bloodshed and more expenditure among his allies? He made one last effort to shore up his power, declaring the political process leading to the Libyan Political Agreement invalid, but he failed to gain support for this assertion.

In Tripoli, the militias, no longer fighting against Haftar, were beginning to confront each other and a small shooting war broke out between two of them. The financial institutions were brought under closer scrutiny and found wanting. Shots were fired at demonstrators protesting in Tripoli against frequent power outages, fuel shortages and general government mismanagement.

In September, Haftar was persuaded that the fair management and distribution of the oil revenue was sufficiently guaranteed and that the loss of revenue if the oil ports remained closed was no longer tolerable. He allowed them to be opened for maintenance and business, and by the middle of October oil sales were getting back to something like normal.

Erdogan's Syrian militias began to go home, and some small signs of optimism began to appear among the governments involved. It is, however, hard to believe that Turkey will give up the concessions in the Eastern Mediterranean gas fields which it fought for, and this will test the patience of Greece, Egypt, Cyprus and others. Neither Turkey nor Libya can escape the economic effects of the Covid-19 pandemic in all its manifestations, and this will make the matter all the more urgent. It will take a great deal of time and effort to resolve.

The Future of Libya

Khalifa Haftar has had a remarkable career. At an age when many people would be reflecting on their past achievements, he was holding an army together. I suspect that he was driven by a vision for the future of his country. There is now the faint glow of hope among those working to settle Libya's future. Of the many pressing problems they must resolve is what to do about the LNA, and by extension Haftar – unless he becomes the strong man and saviour that he has sometimes suggested. There are many military officers in Tripoli who have stated that they will refuse to negotiate with him. Perhaps his hopes will be buried among the mass graves at Tarhuna.

Libya's army, from its foundation in Cairo during the Second World War, can act as a clothesline on which to hang the narrative of Haftar and his country. It helped Emir Idris onto the throne of an independent Libya, and he made sure that it did not help someone to replace him. On his abdication, Muammar Ghaddafi used it to seize power in a putsch. In turn, Ghaddafi also made sure that no ambitious officer would use it to usurp him, and he was willing to kill to guarantee that. His paranoia was lethal, but it helped him stay in power for forty-two years.

The events triggered by the demonstration on the streets of Benghazi in February 2011 have consumed the people and the wealth of Libya in a civil war to which there often seemed no solution. It attracted powerful forces from outside Libya, lured by its oil wealth. Some, whose interpretation of Islam differed markedly from that of Libya's peaceful majority, hijacked the cities and exercised power lethally. The political process has yet to take root. There will be good people wrestling with these and other problems for some time before the matter is settled in favour of ordinary Libyans.

What to do with the armies, and there are a few, must be high on the list of priorities. On 15 October 2020, Haftar held a parade of his LNA on the sand-blown tarmac of his airbase at Jufra. This impressive display of disciplined troops and ample military hardware was aimed both at belligerent foreign forces and at Libyans negotiating for a home-made solution to the nation's problems.

History is too easily written by those who are flattered by it and much too easily eradicated by those who fear it. However, it still has something of value to say. It might inform the deliberations about what to do about Haftar.

We try to quantify military leadership, but most of us recognise that a part of it is unquantifiable and works in context, an important factor when choosing the right person to command an army. When Haftar made his bid for Libya's south, it was a young major in the service of the LNA called Hassan Maatouk, a member of the Awlad Suleiman tribe, who took Sebha for him. Major Maatouk did so without using force but armed with unusual leadership qualities and the prestige of his tribe. He was able to create change without armed conflict in the Libyan context.

Khalifa Haftar has demonstrated his own unusual leadership qualities over a longer period at a higher level, but both he and Maatouk have done so when their particular brand of leadership fitted the circumstances. Will Haftar's leadership qualities work in the new Libya? Major Maatouk will be worth watching.

Haftar made his bid for power at a time when warfare was undergoing a step change and President Erdogan was seeking to prop up the Turkish economy by means of drilling rights in exchange for military help. The odds were then stacked against Haftar. The context was changing. There are, and will be, profound questions about Haftar's leadership before Libya can settle its differences.

AFTERWORD

Too many world powers have occupied Libya. Scattered amongst her modern cities, the coastal oases and the western and the eastern mountains are the remains of Phoenician, Greek, Roman, and Byzantine civilisations which flourished brilliantly in Antiquity and died slowly, leaving the land to Ottoman Turks and Italian colonists. They too had their day and left it all to the Libyans. Now the descendants of the Ottoman Turks and the hard men of a Russian private army face each other across a ceasefire line near the geographical divide which separated Greeks from Romans long ago.

The men of that Russian private army, the Wagner Group, are reportedly constructing a defensive line of ditches and fortifications from west of Sirte to an airfield in the Sahara at Brak al-Shatti. To keep the Turks at bay, or to give President Putin a permanent base in Libya?

Well behind this line and in the east and near Benghazi, a city built close to the remains of ancient Greek Berenice, sits Field Marshal Khalifa Haftar in command of his Libyan National Army. As he strengthens his hold on the east there are signs that the United Nations may have set a viable political process in motion. Will Haftar survive it?

Perhaps his future will soon be determined. Stephanie Williams, the sometime Acting Special Representative of the United Nations

Secretary General in Libya, has catalysed the formation of a new but temporary government which may lead the Libyans into elections on 24 December 2021. It is fervently hoped that the country emerges from the exercise with a government with a strong mandate, but there are pitfalls which might derail the process. It bears some thought.

There appeared recently a force of nature in Libya in the person of Stephanie Williams, an American diplomat not unused to controversy and well versed in the Arab world. Libyan women have been struggling to emerge into public life since the heady days in Benghazi in the early Arab spring but have so far been muted by the violence and aggression which has characterised the exercise of power in Libya for too long. Ms Williams seemed determined that the ballot box should outclass the Kalashnikov in Libyan politics. The vigour with which she set about the job of making that possible was applauded and appreciated by the overwhelmingly male players in Libya's political and military life.

She convened a series of meetings between respected figures in Libyan public life chosen from each of the Fezzan, Cyrenaica and Tripolitania and called the body so formed the Libyan Political Dialogue Forum (LPDF) 'to generate consensus on a unified governance framework and arrangements that will lead to the holding of an election in the shortest possible time frame in order to restore the sovereignty and the democratic legitimacy of Libyan institutions'. She persuaded the LPDF to set 24 December 2021 as the date for a general election in Libya. It had been on that day in 1951 that Libya achieved independence, an event discussed at length in previous chapters of this book.

She is an articulate and forthright diplomat. Here she is being very forthright indeed. She makes the problems Libya faced in December 2020 crystal clear, and the speech is therefore quoted in full.

Afterword

The opening remarks to the seventy-five members attending the virtual meeting of the second round of the Libyan Political Dialogue Forum (LPDF) by Acting UNSMIL head Stephanie Williams on 23rd November 2020

I want to remind you as I said before, time is not on your side. I would like to alert you to the fact that there is a direct cost for inaction and obstruction.

Some indicators I want to alert you to:

1. There now 10 military bases in your country- all over your country – and not in a particular area – that are today either fully are or partially occupied by foreign forces.

2. There are now 20,000 foreign forces and/or mercenaries in your country. That is a shocking violation of Libyan sovereignty. You may believe that these foreigners are here as your guests, but they are now occupying your house. This is a blatant violation of the arms embargo.

3. They are here pouring weapons into your country, a country which does not need more weapons.

4. They are not in Libya for your interests, they are in Libya for their interests.

'*Dirou balkom*' [take care]. You have now a serious crisis with regard to the foreign presence in your country.

I have previously warned you about the declining socioeconomic conditions in the country and the fact that we expect in one month time, exactly in January 2021, there will be 1.3 million Libyans, your compatriots, your citizens in need of humanitarian assistance.

There is a sharp decline in the purchasing power of the Libyan Dinar. The liquidity crisis has fully returned. There is a shortage of cash in circulation.

There is a terrible electricity crisis now. I don't need to remind you of how terrible the electricity shortages were last summer. Because of the terrible corruption and the mis-governance, all over the country. I am not pointing fingers. This is a crisis in the West and in the East. You have a crisis of corruption. You have a mis-governance crisis and now you have only 13 of 27 powerplants that are functioning.

One billion US dollars is needed immediately to be invested in the electrical infrastructure in order to avert a complete collapse of the electrical grid in your country.

This is very difficult now because of the divisions in the institutions, and because of the epidemic of corruption and this kleptocratic class that is determined to remain in power.

This is accompanied by a deepening COVID-19 crisis. You now have almost 94,000 COVID-19 cases in Libya. We think those estimates are low and that the actual number is higher, but there is a terrible shortage of testing in the country.

You have foreign actors who are behaving with complete impunity. You have domestic actors who are engaging in widespread corruption, self-dealing and mismanagement of the country. You have an increasing lack of accountability and human rights problems on a daily basis. We are getting reports of kidnapping, arbitrary detentions, killings by armed groups all over the country.

While there is a lot of political tourism going to different countries and capitals, the average Libyans are suffering, and the indications of improvement for their situation are not there.

We believe – and I think many of you believe – that the best way to move forward is through this political dialogue. This is a broad and inclusive forum for decision-making and people are counting on you. We went a long way (at our last meeting) in Tunis. We set the date of elections. We need to hold all those institutions that need to produce the elections accountable, but you also have a governance crisis. The best way to address your governance crisis is to unify your institutions, to unify your Central Bank which needs to have a board meeting to address the exchange rate crisis immediately.

I know that there are many who think that this whole dialogue is just about sharing power, but it is really about sharing responsibility for future generations. This is my ask of you as we have the discussions today in going forward, because, and I will say it again, time is not on your side.

The deliberations, skilfully guided by Ms Williams, concluded with the decision to raise a Government of National Unity (GNU) through the auspices of the LPDF which reflected a fair representation from each of the provinces, as far as that was possible. This superseded the Government of National Accord, a body that had signally failed to govern. The GNU was tasked with selecting a committee charged with writing a new constitution before the ballot takes place.

The GNU obtained the formal approval of a quorate House of Representatives, Libya's remaining elected legislative authority but which has been divided for too long. It was to undertake, as its first priority, the preparations for and the administration of the ballot on 24 December 2021 and, in order to forestall accusations of regional bias, was to make Sirte its seat of power.

All candidates for the new GNU undertook to hold national presidential and parliamentary elections on the date specified, and in which they will not stand for office. They also promised to appoint women to 30 percent of senior government roles.

But they also decided that there could be no elections without a settled constitution and that may yet prove a sticking point. Firstly, is it to be a secular constitution? Or will it be hijacked my militant Islamists and become bogged down in arguments about the place Sharia Law is to play in the constitution?

A further difficulty may be obtaining approval from Libya's ethnic minorities. The Amazigh (Berbers and Tuaregs) and Tebu ethnic minorities have so far refused to approve a draft constitution hammered together some time ago. There will be plenty of opportunities to cause delays.

What is Haftar's potential role in the proposed democratic process? He still has effective power in the east of Libya and considerable influence in southern Libya. In stark terms, and at the time of writing, the political process is unlikely to proceed in the east without Haftar's cooperation – or his death or deposition – for the simple reason that no election can be held in the east unless he facilitates it. Why? Because he has consolidated his hold over key units in the LNA and brought his army to the aid of the civil power.

He has replaced ineffective local governments with effective military leaders and has successfully courted powerful tribal leaders who have helped him control swaths of inhospitable territory. In this way he has been able to keep his logistical support in operation over great distances. His propaganda machine is effective and he has an instinct for fuelling and harnessing popular paranoia. However, his Libyan National Army is a coalition held together by the power of his personality. Can he survive? And will he cooperate in the political process?

There were two incidents in my life in Libya which brought me into contact with the parallel world in which great deals were, and perhaps still are, made in the oil business. One of them put me in some physical danger, and the other placed me in some moral danger. In the latter I was complicit but I claim in mitigation that my role was peripheral and rather petty. I cannot claim even the smallest experience of the armament industry, though I was trained to use some of its products. Why is this relevant?

It leads me to include the full text of Ms William's address to Libyan Political Dialogue Forum (LPDF) in this Afterword and ask – as has the reader I am sure – why she was able to spell out Libya's problems with such devastating clarity when others have failed to do so. The second question her address poses is this: if the problems she outlines were so easily observed and corroborated by her, is it likely that international governments were unaware of them? Surely not.

The reason they were silent might be sought in the oil fields of Libya and the opportunities to share some of the great wealth they contain. Perhaps potential access to it may have led them to exercise excessive diplomacy. The internationally recognised Government of National Accord was clearly not governing Libya. Could it have traded access to its wealth for the benefits of high office?

Amongst the remaining issues which have involved Haftar in Libya's future is the distribution of the oil wealth amongst the Libyan people, a matter which has been a cause of considerable discord. It has been associated with the possibility of corruption and misgovernance. Haftar has persuaded the eastern and southern tribes to support his efforts to clean up the mess. Even if he is toppled from the command of the LNA, his efforts to see that an equitable distribution of Libya's oil wealth is established must be recognised.

Which returns us to the matter of corruption. It must be amongst the most pressing problems faced by those who would settle Libya's issues. Here is the courageous Stephanie Williams addressing the matter head on when she spoke to the British newspaper *The Guardian*:

> [In Libya] Their numbers numerically are not significant, but there is a constituency of the status quo. The existing political class are not interested in committing class suicide. They see any change through a temporary executive or to national elections as an end to their privileged access to the coffers, and resources of the state, and so it would put an end to their system of patronage that they have so adeptly developed in the past few years.

Elections are a direct threat to their status quo, and they are going
to fight to defend their status quo, and it's my belief that those are
trying to block the formation of a consensual unified executive are
the very same political forces that will try to block elections.

King Idris struggled with corruption. Ghaddafi joined the
gang as the supreme beneficiary. Any future government of Libya
attempting to eliminate ingrained and all-pervading corruption
will be faced with a classic dilemma – whether to fight it or join
it. Allowing the rampant pillage of Libya's resources by what
Williams calls the kleptocracy has a sad but practical merit in that
it maintains what stability remains. Fighting it, on the other hand,
upsets an already fragile equilibrium.

A government bent on clearing up the tragic mess will need a
very strong mandate indeed and the support of an independent
and incorruptible civil service and judiciary. At the time of writing
that seems unlikely.

It is important to rehearse once again the problem posed by the
Tripoli militias which have not been integrated into a civil police
force or a standing army. They have remained as private armies
under the command of ruthless and powerful leaders and have
infiltrated the machinery of government and exercised a malign,
probably crippling, influence on the United Nations-recognised
Government of National Accord.

Now that they are no longer fighting against Haftar they have
time to concentrate on profitable enterprises, amongst which is
people trafficking. The consensus of views about the treatment
of migrants is disturbing. The burgeoning lawlessness has given
energy to cruel and racist traits in Libya which shame its leaders
and those who profit from the traffic in human beings. What part
could Haftar play in this most pressing of problems? There are
many powerful Tripolitanian militia leaders who have expressed
their opposition to him emphatically. How well entrenched are

these militia leaders? Could they eat their words without a side serving of compensation for loss of earnings?

In the meantime, what has Haftar been doing? He has been building his LNA into an effective fighting force and preparing it for a 'fight to the death' with Turkey, which has become the significant military power in Tripolitania.

We can discern a careful plan behind all his actions. He has cranked up his propaganda machine and displayed his disciplined Libyan National Army in impressive parades and ceremonials. He has promoted his loyal officers and made a public display of doing so, receiving their gratitude with carefully controlled dignity and ceremony. He has held exercises in the hinterlands with live firing and realistic objectives. In so doing he has demonstrated his power, military hardware and the effectiveness of his army in field exercises both to potential enemies and wavering allies. He has cultivated the leaders of the respected tribes and rewarded the Awaquir in Benghazi in particular.

Most significant of all, he has brought his army to the aid of the civil powers as far south as Kufra, and particularly in Benghazi. In this he has made himself the effective civil power in East Libya. He has, like many leaders in history, chosen an enemy which he can use to rouse his wavering and his loyal allies.

On 25 December 2020, during a speech at a parade near Benghazi celebrating the sixty-ninth anniversary of Libya's independence, Field Marshal Khalifa Haftar delivered a speech in which he declared, 'We are prepared for war against Turkey.' The *Libya Address Journal* of that date published the main points he made. The journal is part of Haftar's propaganda machine and should be viewed with due caution.

Independence has no value, freedom has no meaning, no security, no peace, while the feet of the Turkish army contaminate our pure land. There is no choice for the occupying enemy. Unless they leave peacefully and voluntarily or by force of arms and strong will ... The era of your (Turkish) colonial illusions is over, and you must choose whether to leave or war ... Turkey and its mercenaries are continuing to mobilize for the war, a war in which if the first bullet is fired in it, let them prepare for certain death ... The aggressor did not stop sending mercenaries and weapons of all kinds, declaring war on the Libyans, defying the Libyan will, and underestimating human values ... There is no peace in the shadow of the coloniser, and with his presence on our land, we will take up arms to make peace in our hands and with our free will ... We will make it with our heroic army that knows nothing but victory and chased terrorists from Benghazi and the south until they took refuge among the people of Tripoli.

We must assume that Haftar would have chosen his words with care. He does not do rabble-rousing. He speaks quietly and with purpose. Who was Haftar addressing in this speech? He was giving his troops a purpose – a purposeless army is likely to disintegrate. Haftar's army is a coalition and he was welding it together by offering a common enemy to the regional and Islamist militias and the powerful officers within it who harboured private ambitions. He was sending signals to his civilian friends and enemies using Libya's history as a propaganda weapon. He was sending a message to President Sisi of Egypt and to the leadership of the United Arab Emirates whoes support is crucial, as we have seen. He was setting out a 'non plus ultra' line of defence to President Erdogan and the leaders of Qatar. But there will be those who ask if Haftar was indulging in dangerous brinkmanship. His speech looks bellicose in the light of recent signs of rapprochement amongst hitherto sworn enemies in the Arab world – especially so as there are signs of a reconciliation of sorts between Turkey and Egypt after a seven-year standoff which began when Turkey backed the ill-fated Egyptian Muslim

Brotherhood-aligned President Mohammed Morsi in 2012. Morsi was deposed by Sisi the following year.

What of Erdogan and his Libyan adventure now? Much has been said in this book about President Erdogan's aggressive intervention in Libya which has focused on his need to access the natural gas bonanza below the Eastern Mediterranean. There is no need to rehearse that again in detail but there is room to suggest that he may catch his toe in Libya because of the nature of Libyans. There is no guarantee that Libya will end the violence and survive as a unified state. The glue that holds the old provinces together, which should maintain the territorial integrity and political unity of the nation, has never been all that strong and has been tested – perhaps beyond repair. Libya may divide into two or more entities. It is easy to despair at this, but the United Kingdom is struggling to remain united and has many more years of unity behind it than Libya.

Are the Turks risking entanglement in a failed state at the far end of a tenuous supply line, and exacerbating their already fractious relations with Greece, Cyprus, Egypt and Israel? The relationship between Turkey and these countries may deteriorate so far as to force the latter into a military alliance at worst or to combine to squeeze Turkey out of their combined economic zones. Though this is not immediately likely, Erdogan could precipitate it by his belligerence.

In the matter of Haftar and Egypt there has been a new, more cautious approach by the latter following a slight but interesting easing of tension in the Middle East. Even so, the Egyptians cannot afford to have Turkey entrenched in their western neighbourhood. So, they have established extensive military bases within easy reach of Libya's eastern border. That gives them a marginal advantage against the otherwise better-equipped, more proficient and better-led Turkish military. Turkey, however, is also stretched by other conflicts, especially in Syria where it is fending off the formation of a Kurdish state.

In Libya especially, forming a new government without a political mandate cannot be easy. The GNU, for its part, is attempting to satisfy a number of interests in the appointments of ministers: regional and tribal interests, matters of gender equality, and the concerns of *thuwwars* and militias. In light of this balancing act, the prime minister will inevitably be denied the services of some people of competence and independence.

But the new government has been granted a short life and one major objective: to prepare and execute a fair and democratic election. The Libyan people, by now somewhat disappointed in governments, will not expect much else. The hardest problem to solve will be to get a new constitution drafted and accepted in a national referendum before elections are held.

There remains the pressing matter of extreme Islamic Jihadists in Libya and the threat they pose to neighbouring countries. As we have discussed, both IS and al-Qaeda in the Islamic Maghreb have made efforts to establish themselves in Libya. Furthermore, it is notable that the lethal jihadists of Boko Haram are making alarming inroads into neighbouring Burkina Faso and causing havoc in northern Nigeria. They are doing so with arms looted from Ghaddafi's armouries.

Haftar has made a stand against the Muslim Brotherhood as he seems to feel that they would offer a sympathetic ear to the proponents of jihad. Libya's neighbour, Egypt, would resist a Muslim Brotherhood-aligned government on its western borders and has threatened to intervene if Turkey, whose government is seen as Muslim Brotherhood Lite, were to advance its forces into East Libya.

It is unlikely that the remains of Ansar al-Sharia, driven out of Benghazi and Derna by Haftar, and the likes of al-Qaeda in the Islamic Maghreb, who thrive in the remote Badlands, have vanished miraculously. It is noted that Haftar's forces destroyed a nest of al-Qaeda fighters in Obari in November 2020. There must be more, and there are plenty of places where they can hole up.

In passing, it is hard to claim that the Islamist jihadists who terrorised Benghazi, Derna and Sirte were desirable governors to ordinary citizens. If Haftar had not removed them, someone else would have had to.

The place of militant Islam in politics remains a critical issue for any future government of Libya and for much of the rest of the Islamic world. It will take time and effort to reconcile those jihadists who harbour such a powerful sense of anger against the secular or moderate majority. In the end, the best minds in the Islamic world will have to find a solution to the problem and the non-Islamic world must look more closely at its attitudes and assumptions about a faith which is going through considerable self-examination and spreading rapidly still. Haftar, we must remind ourselves, is a proponent of secular government and he will stand firm as such. Is that what the Libyans want? Is there anyone else who has the will and the resources to make that happen?

Does Western-style democracy stand a chance in modern Libya? In a paper entitled 'The Role of Tribal Dynamics in the Libyan Future', Arturo Varvelli of the Italian Institute for International Political Studies proposes a near-unique trilemma which the people of Libya must somehow resolve in order to function as a nation. As I understand it, he argues that the coexistence of Islam, democracy and a rentier state has never been successful.

It is, he seems to argue, possible to implement only *some* democratic principles in an Islamic state. I too argue that in practice the separation of Islam from popular democracy is not easy to achieve. Both the Holy Koran and the authenticated sayings of the Prophet Mohamed contained in the Sunna are silent on the matter of representational 'Western' democracy. Some Muslims argue that the democratic process has its roots in 'Shura' or consultation. The growing Salafist movement, however, rejects all such debate, arguing that what is not accounted for in the core texts is un-Islamic and thus outlawed.

Arturo Varvelli argues that the rentier state – one which derives most of its income from rents paid by foreign individuals or governments, particularly to extract oil and gas – does not encourage democracy. He and others suggest that rentier states do not need to tax their people, who consequently have no incentive to exert pressure on government to respond to their needs. We might upend the inspirational catch phrase of the American War of Independence – no taxation without representation – and suggest, only party humorously, that democracy withers unless citizens have a personal stake in their government.

The examples of Gulf states such as Qatar, the United Arab Emirates and Saudi Arabia tend to show that a rentier state which is at the same time an Islamic state cannot also be truly democratic. The common factor that these states share is the presence, so far at least, of a hereditary ruling family: the House of Al Thani in Qatar, the eponymous Ibn Saud, and in the UAE, Al Nahyan and Al Makhtoum amongst others. Gaddafi's efforts to establish himself and his family in a similar role in Libya failed spectacularly in 2011, probably because of his serious character flaws, the low esteem in which his tribe is held and his suppression of Libya's fundamental Islamists.

It would seem then that the brave attempt to hold a general election on 24 December 2021 may not resolve the Libyan trilemma. But Varvelli's hypothesis, persuasive as it is, is not the only one available.

If you have not lived, or at least travelled widely, in Libya, you will have but a theoretical appreciation of its size and consequently the profound isolation its people lived with until the oil wealth brought the great majority of them to live in the coastal cities. The isolation was exacerbated by the Italian colonists who excluded Libyans from Western education and thus the chance to accumulate knowledge, skills and intellectual capital. When independence arrived in 1951 – within my lifetime, to make the point clear – Libya's intellectual capital was negligible and thus supplied by foreigners. Whilst this deficit is being repaired – there is no intelligence deficit – there is another problem. There is also a political deficit, which was made even more acute by the erratic domination of Libyan life for forty or so years by Muammar Ghaddafi. I argue that these are amongst the reasons why Libya was different to Egypt, where the Arab Spring reached a tolerable settlement relatively quickly. It should be said that Ghaddafi's huge 'Armoury of Islam', when looted, supplied Libyans with the arms to prolong the turmoil.

Some mistakes are easy to see in hindsight. Perhaps a crucial one was made by NATO as far back as 2011. It was predictable; the NATO intervention which hastened the removal of Muammar Ghaddafi was undertaken in haste and without the benefit of good advice. The attempt by Saif al-Islam al-Ghaddafi to ameliorate the repressive reign of his father led to the release of a number of extreme Islamist prisoners from the notorious Abu Salim gaol. Both actions had unforeseen consequences, the first because the desirable removable of Ghaddafi shattered Libya. Why?

First of all, NATO, conscious of the aftermath of the war in Iraq, withdrew and left Libya to deal with the consequences arising. The rebel National Transition Council was unable to govern, and Libya slid into civil war. Secondly, the extremists, taking advantage the power vacuum left by Ghaddafi's demise, formed militias and imposed their will on Benghazi, Derna and Sirte, turning them into havens for IS and al-Qaeda.

Khalifa Haftar fought long and bloody battles to remove the Islamist jihadists from Benghazi and Derna. He was successful in the end and he was tempted to go for Tripoli. He gave clear notice of his intentions and there was a time when Fayez al-Serraj, head of the UN-recognised GNA, might have attempted to negotiate with him. But al-Serraj had closed the door on talks with Haftar emphatically and publicly. He could not eat his words, it seems. To blame Haftar solely for intransigent behaviour is too easy.

Despite this, Haftar's surprise attack on Libya's capital was, in my view at least, his great misjudgement. When his army arrived at the gates of Tripoli, he clearly expected discontented Tripoli militias to come over to his side. They did not, and so Haftar was forced to attack the city without them and attempt to grind his way into its vitals. There may have been a time when he could have sued for an advantageous peace. Perhaps he thought he could win. He overlooked the belligerent determination of President Erdogan, who saw Haftar was overextended, went for his throat and pushed him out of Tripolitania.

It is pertinent to ask how many died in the battles for Tripoli because the answer will have a bearing on Libya's future. We can bet there were many. Some sources say that 1,048 were killed and 5,558 wounded in the four months spanning from April to July 2020. Some say that over 2,356 were killed altogether. It will be more than that.

Khalifa Belqasim Haftar is a long way from Ouadi Doum. How much further will he go?

SELECT BIBLIOGRAPHY

Briggs, Lloyd Cabot, *Tribes of the Sahara* (Cambridge, Mass: Harvard University Press, 1960)

Cagapty, Soner, *Erdogan's Empire, Turkey and the Politics of the Middle East* (London: I.B. Tauris, 2020)

Crowley, Roger, *Empires of the Sea, The Final Battle for the Mediterranean, 1521-1580* (London: Faber Co Ltd, 2008)

Dearden, Seton, *A Nest of Corsairs, The Fighting Karamanlis of the Barbary Coast* (London: John Murray, 1976)

De Angostini, Enrico, *Le Popolazioni della Cireniaca* (Benghazi: Governo della Cireniaca, 1922)

Epstein, Edward J., *Dossier, the Secret History of Armand Hammer* (London: Orion Business Books, 1988)

Esposito, John (Ed.), *The Oxford History of Islam* (Oxford University Press, 1999)

Dear, I. C. B. and Foot, M. R. D. (Consultant Ed.), *The Oxford Companion to WWII* (Oxford University Press, 1995)

Evans-Pritchard, E. E., *The Senusi of Cyrenaica* (Oxford University Press, 1973)

Forbes, Rosita, *The Secret of the Sahara: Kufra* (London: Cassell and Company, 1921)

Ghaddafi, Muammar and Jouve, Edmund, *My Vision* (London: John Blake, 2005)

Hassanein, A. M., *The Lost Oases* (London: Thornton Butterworth, 1925)

Holmboe, Knud, *Desert Encounter* (London: The Quilliam Press, 1994)

Kelly, Saul, *War and Politics in the Desert* (London: Silphium Press, 2010)

Mango, Andrew, *Ataturk* (London: John Murray, 1999)

Mansfield, Peter, *The Arabs* (London: Penguin Books, 1981)

Oakes, John, *Libya The History of Ghaddafi's Pariah State* (Stroud: The History Press, 2011)

Osman, Tarek, *Egypt on the Brink, From Nasser to the Muslim Brotherhood* (Yale University Press, 2013)

Pack, Jason (Ed.), *The 2011 Libyan Uprisings and the Struggle for the Post-Quadhafi Future* (New York: Palgrave Macmillan, 2013)

Pargeter, Alison, *The Muslim Brotherhood from Opposition to Power* (London: Saqi Books, 2014)

Peters, Emrys L., *The Bedouin of Cyrenaica* (Cambridge University Press, 1900)

Pollack, Kenneth M., *Arabs at War, Military Effectiveness, 1948–1991* (University of Nebraska Press, 2002)

Pollock, Douglas, *The Conquest of the Sahara* (Oxford University Press, 1984)

Wright, John, *Libya, Chad and the Central Sahara* (London: Hurst and Company, 1989)

ACKNOWLEDGEMENTS

This book is in part payment of the debt I owe those colleagues and friends with whom I shared more than eight years of my life in Libya. My late wife, June, lived those years with me and our daughter, Nikki, was born there. June loved Tripoli and I know she would have thanked her colleagues and friends in that city had she lived to do so. I do so now on her behalf.

The mistakes and omissions in this book are mine alone. No editor could be expected to eliminate all the errors of judgement or the failures of memory.

Sophie Bradshaw consented to be my literary agent and did her best to make the project attractive to a publisher and also give me a crash course in book writing. She has a keen eye for meritorious verbiage much of which, thankfully, she eliminated. She deserves my thanks. It was a difficult job which she did well.

Connor Stait was brave enough to commission this book for Amberley. We both hope that it offers its readers some insights into the seemingly endless troubles that have beset the Libyan people for too long.

Alex Bennett has been my copy-editor at Amberley. Those who write books will acknowledge the crucial work that copy-editors do to improve their writing. They do this in private and must content themselves with a small paragraph, such as this, in the author's acknowledgements. The best of them, and Alex is amongst that talented group, take pleasure in the subtle but crucial improvements they make and, eventually, the emergence of their book in print. I am responsible for the errors, not Alex.

There are others I want to thank. They will know why. First amongst them are those friends in the RAF and the oil industry amongst whom my wife and I lived and worked in Tripoli and Benghazi. They may be scattered around the world or still living in the turmoil that has been visited on Libya.

Whilst writing *War Lord* I was coached from the side-lines by many friends, some of whom I tested beyond the conventions of friendship with frequent reports on its progress. Amongst that forbearing and consistently positive group are Colin Brooks, John MacDonald, Bill Dance, Roland Denning, Kim Slater and Terry and Bill Harvey.

When this work was nearing its end the support I recived from Mia Foster was crucial and given unstintingly. Nikki and Becky Mitchell were there all the time.

John Oakes
Libyastories.com

INDEX

Abaidat (Tribe) (*aka Obeidat*), 65

Abu Abbas, 100

Abu Nidal, 100

Abu Salim gaol, 116

Abu Salim Families (Benghazi), 116

Abushagur, Dr Mustafa, 147

Abu Ubaida ibn al-Jarrah Brigade, implicated in the murder of General Fatah Younis al Obeidi, 128

Ajdabiya 22, 24, 26, 82, 119, 123, 155, geographical and strategic significance 27, Khalifa Haftar's birthplace 42

al-Banna, Hassan, Founder of the Muslim Brotherhood, 54

al-Barani, Ashkal, 134

al-Dam, Ahmed Ghadaf, Brigadier, Libyan intelligence officer, 111-112

al-Feitouri, General Mohamed Hadia, assassinated in Benghazi, 147

al-Hasadi, Abdul-Hakim, 129

al-Jazeera media empire, selective reporting by, 141, sets up Libya al-Ahrar TV station, 141

al-Libi, Abou Yahya, al-Qaeda second-in-command, death of, 150, 159

al-Maghrabi, Mahmud Sulayman, 70

al-Obeidi, Staff General Abdul Fatah Younis (*aka Younis*), 122, 135, arrives in Benghazi, 118, suspected of collusion with Ghaddafi's son, 123, 127-128, murdered, 128

al-Qaeda, training camp in Derna, 158

Al Thani, Sheik Abdul Hamed
  bin Khalifa, Emir of Qatar,
  connections with Libya, 141
Al-Zuetina, 155, 228
Alexandria, 30
Anderson, Norman, 55
Anglo-Egyptian Treaty,
  abrogated 51
Ansar al-Sharia, and US
  ambassador Stevens, 150,
  151, street demonstration
  against in Benghazi, 151, 152,
  other branches of, 152, in
  Derna, 156
Aouzou Strip, 79, 82
Arab Spring, 114–116, unique in
  Libya, 116
Arsenal of Islam, 102
Awaquir (Tribe) 23, 28, 65
Awlad Suleman (Tribe) 27, 44,
  76

Bab al-Aziziya, 94, 96, 98, 134,
  136
Bani Walid 44, siege of, 139–140
Barclays Dominion, Colonial and
  Overseas Bank, 74
Belmokhtar, Mokhtar, al-Qaeda
  in the Islamic Maghreb,
  operates in Libya, 161
Belhaj, Abdelhakim, 113, 136,
  139, 141, his militia in
  Tripoli, 145

Ben Amer, Huda, sometime
  Mayor of Benghazi, 118, 147
Ben Qumu, Sufian, Islamist war
  lord in Derna, 156
Beni Hilal (Tribes) 27, 28
Beni Sulaim (Tribes) 28
Benghazi 20, 21, 95, 98, 123,
  124, and the Arab Spring, 117
Benina 22, 98
Bevin–Sforza Plan, 60
Blair, Tony, British Prime
  Minister, meets Ghaddafi near
  Sirte, 113, implications of the
  meeting discussed, 113
Blue Mountain, British security
  company guarding US
  consulate in Benghazi, 149
Bouazizi, Mohamed, self
  immolates and triggers the
  Arab Spring, 114
British Military presence in the
  Kingdom of Libya, 64
British Military Administration,
  of Cyrenaica 26, 27, of
  Tripolitania 53, 55, 58
British Military Mission to
  Libya, 48
Bromilow, Lieutenant Colonel,
  British founding commander
  of the Libyan Arab Force, 38

Cabot Briggs, Lloyd, 82
Cairo 36

Cameron, David, British Prime
Minister, 126
Chad 19, 29, 35, 76, 78, 80, and
the Tebu 58
CIA, 92, 93, 97, 102, 106, CIA
HQ Langley, 110, operatives
in Benghazi when Ambassador
Stevens was killed, 148
Clinton, Hillary, US Secretary
of State, meets Mohamed
Jebril, 126, in the matter of
Ambassador Stevens, 149
Commonwealth War Graves
Commission, WWII cemetery
in Benghazi vandalised by
Islamist militia, 146
Cyrenaica (*see also East Libya*)
22, 24, 26, tribes of 37,
internal self-government
achieved, 60
Cyrenaican Defence Force, 57,
66, 69, 112
Cumming, Sir Duncan, Chief
Administrator BMA of
Cyrenaica, education, 26, early
problems with food shortages
27, 57, politicises the Senussi
Order 57

Darfur, 35, 82
Dawn Mermaid, Operation,
against Ghaddafi in Tripoli,
134

Dearlove, Sir Richard, justifies
the meeting between Tony
Blair and Ghaddafi, 114
Déby, Idriss, sometime president
of Chad, 91
Derna, Khalifa Haftar at school
in 42, militant Islamists in,
129, 156-158, executions in,
158
Djamous, Hassan 83-84, tactics
in the Toyota Wars, 84,
attacks Fada 85-86, captures
Ouadi Doum, 87, captures
Maatan al Sarra, 87
Dorda, Abuzayd, Libyan
Ambassador to the UN, 1997
2003, 111

Eden, Anthony, British Foreign
Secretary, 40
Egypt, 30, 31

Fada, 85
Farjan (Tribe), homeland and
influence 29
Farouk, King of Egypt, 37, 51
Fawaqir (Tribe) 28
Faya Largo, 85, 108
Fezzan 23, 82, Free French
administration of, 26, 27, 53,
58, 59
Fletcher, Yvonne, 97
Forbes, Rosita, 82

France, fall of in WWII 38
Free French 23, 58
Free Officers (Libya) 48

General National Congress,
    mooted, 121, threats of
    violence against, 153
Ghaddadfa (Tribe) 28, 44
Ghadames, 59, 161
Ghaddafi, al-Saadi, 117, 136
Ghaddafi Brigades, 112
Ghaddafi, Khamis, commands
    Khamis Brigade, 134, 136
Ghaddafi, Muammar, 35, 64, 69,
    70, birth near Sirte 32, 33,
    his Green Book 44, purchases
    arms from Russia and Soviet
    Bloc, 74, military dispositions
    and strength, 75, military
    shortcomings, 75, and Chad
    78, 79, 84, foreign policy 78,
    79, survived coups in 1975,
    85, betrays and abandons
    Haftar, 91-92, personality
    cult, 95, persecutes dissidents
    overseas, 97, relations with
    the USA, 98-102, volte face
    on Libyan POWs in Chad,
    110, meets Tony Blair, 113,
    armouries looted, 118, forces
    available to confront rebels
    in 2011, 124, treatment of
    ethnic minorities, 133, defeat
in Tripoli, 134-136, last stand
    in Sirte, 136, beaten to death,
    137, demise leaves a power
    vacuum, 143–144
Ghaddafi, Mu'atassem,
    commands Ghedaffi's forces
    on the Brega front, 128,
    136, defends father in Sirte,
    136-137, dies in suspicious
    circumstances, 137
Ghaddafi, Saif al-Islam, 114,
    captured by Zintani militia,
    136
Gharian (city), 135
Ghat, 59, 161, 212, 213
Grand Senussi (see also Senussi)
    31
Graziani, General Rodolfo, Vice
    Governor of Libya 24
Great Man-made River, 158
Gulf of Sirte (aka Gulf of Sidra)
    27, 155

Habré, Hissene, sometime
    President of Chad, 76, 83,
    alliance with Goukouni
    Oueddei, 88, relations with
    Ronald Regan, 90, 101, and
    Libyan prisoners of war, 91,
    106
Haftar Khalifa, birth, 27, his tribe,
    and its connections, 29, 30,
    early career, 76–78, training

in leadership in the USSR, 77, commanding in Chad, 80–82, 84, captured at Ouadi Doum, 88–89, joins National Front for the Salvation of Libya (NFSL), 105, forms the Libyan National Army in Chad, 105, accusations of Human Rights violations, 107, accused of mistreating Libyan POWs in Chad, 106–107, accused of using chemical weapons in Chad, 108-109, in the USA, 109–112, breaks with the NFSL, 113, granted US citizenship, 113, returns to Libya, 114, as Field Marshal 35

Hariri, Omar, member of the NTC with the military portfolio, 122

Healy, Dennis, British politician, 70

Human Rights Watch, 92, 106, 109, reports on the massacre of Ghaddafi supporters near Sirte, 137-138, reports on the detention of migrant workers, 138

Idris al-Senussi, King of Libya (*see also Senussi*) 31, 34, 57, 61, called the Shepherd

King, 64, prefers Tobruk, 65, control of Armed Forces, 67, plagued by corruption, 67, abdicates, 67, death, 68

Interim National Council (INC), 121, 125, formed in Benghazi, 120, main members, 120, forces available to confront Ghaddafi, 123, fails to control Tripoli militias, 139

International Organisation for Migration, reports on detention of migrant workers by militias, 137–138

Islamic Association of Libya, 97

Islamic Legion, in Chad, 83, 93, 100, 101

Italy, 10th Army of invades Egypt, 25

Jadhran, Ibrahim, commander of Petroleum Facilities Guard in Libya's Oil Crescent, 154, shuts down Ras Lanuf, al-Sidra oil ports, 155, forms Libyan Oil and Gas Corporation, 155

Jalil, Mustafa Abdul, chair of rebel Interim National Council, 120, 135

Jalloud, Major Abdul Salem, 99, 189

Jebel Akhdar (aka Green
Mountains) 28
Jebel Nefusa (aka Western
Mountains) 35
Jebril, Mohamed, 125, 126

Kenya, 110
Khan, Dr Abdul Qadeer,
Pakistani nuclear scientist, 98
Kufra, 28, 29, 82, 154, clashes
between Tebu and Zawiya
tribe in, 158

Lampson, Sir Milles, British
Ambassador to Egypt 37
Leclerc, Free French General 26,
59
Lévy, Bernard-Henry, brokers
meeting between President
Sarkozy and rebels, 124,
connection with N. Sarkozy,
125
Libyan Arab Force, raised in
Egypt 35–39, role in the
future of Libya, 39, 40, 41,
57, first deployment in Libya
40, 55
Libyan Army, performance in
Chad, 88-89, prisoners of
war in Chad, 91, military
competence, 100, in Chad,
102–104

Libyan Change and Reform
Movement, 113
Libyan Constitutional Union, 96,
97
Libyan Embassy, London, 97
Libyan Democratic National
Rally, 97
Libyan Independence
Negotiations, 59–62
Libyan Islamic Fighting Group,
112, 135, 139
Libyan National Army, LNA,
109, 112, 113
Libyan National Oil
Corporation, 155
Libya's porous borders discussed,
159–161
Lough, Ted, British Army Officer
commanding the British
Military Mission to Libya,
49, 70
Lugard, Sir Fredrick, and Indirect
Rule, 56

Magariaf, Dr Mohmad Youssef,
94, 96, president of Congress
in August 2012, 146
Magharba (Tribe) 23, 24, 28, 94,
155, 156
Marabtin (*client tribes*),
relationship to Sa'adi tribes, 28,
29, 95, Marabtin bil baraka
(*tribes of the blessing*) 29

Marsa Brega 22, 24, 123, 127, 128

Médecins Sans Frontières, stops work in protest about torture, 132

MI5, 97

MI6, 114

militias, aka *Thuwwars*, 119, post-revolutionary militias formed after Ghaddafi's regime collapses, 144–145

Misrata, Ghaddafi at school in 45, 94–98, street protest triggers war, 130, anti-Ghaddafi militias formed, 131, urban warfare in, 131, in battle for Tripoli, 135, militias lay siege to Bani Walid, 139–140, some militias accused of torture, 145, brigades threaten a military coup in Tripoli, 153–154

Misratan Union of Revolutionaries, 132

Mohammed, General Suleiman, the head of the 8th Army Tobruk joins the INC in 2011, 124

Montgomery, Bernard, British 8th Army Commander, 26

Morsi, Mohammed, President of Egypt 2012–2013, 105

Mursa Matruh, 110

Murzuq, 83, 159, 162, 210, 212, 213, 227

Muslim Brotherhood 31, 32, 37, 54, 105, 112

Mussolini, Benito, Italian fascist dictator, 23, 25, 26

Naker, Abdullah Ahmed, powerful leader of Tripoli militias, 145

Nasser, Gamal Abdul 32, 47, 49, 50, 64, 105, some biographical details of 51

National Oil Corporation (Libya) 19

National Front for the Salvation of Libya, 92, 93, 97, 104, Haftar and, 104, 112

National Transitional Council, 125, 128, NATO loses confidence in, 135

NATO, 74, no-fly zone commences, 127, involvement in war increases, 130, 134, withdraws when Ghaddafi killed, 141, leaves a power vacuum in Libya, 141

N'Djamena, 94

Neguib, Muhammad, Egyptian Army General, President of Egypt 1952, 52

Niger, 82

Oil and Gas Council, Libyan, 96
Omar Mukhtar 25
Ottoman Turks 23, 63
Ouadi Doum 20, 76, 80, 81,
    85, 86-87, Libyan military
    performance at 87, 93, 102
Oueddei, Goukouni, sometime
    President of Chad, 76, 83,
    alliance with Habré, 88, 108

Pan American World Airways
    flight 103 (Lockerbie), 101
Pelt, Adrian, UN High
    Commissioner for Libya,
    61, promotes a National
    Assembly, 61
Pentagon, Assessment of
    Ghaddafi's vulnerability, 85
Petroleum Facilities Guard, 154,
    155
Political Bureau of Cyrenaica,
    155–156
Potsdam Conference, 59

Qaid, Abdul Wahab Hassain,
    and Libya's porous southern
    border, 159–161
Qatar, forces in Tripoli, 134,
    influence of its media
    136, implications of its
    involvement in Libya, 140,
    supplies NTC with arms and

special service advisors, 141,
    long-term aims for Libya, 142

Ras Lanuf, 119, 123, 124, 155
Reagan, Ronald, 76, 109, and
    Chad, 84, and Ghaddafi,
    85, 100, 104, sees Haftar
    as a potential asset, 87,
    98, Reagan Doctrine, 98,
    launches punishing air raid on
    Ghaddafi, 99
Revolutionary Command
    Council (Libya) 48, 69, 70
Rommel, Erwin (General), 22,
    23, 55, 76, 84, 127
Royal Libyan Military Academy,
    Benghazi 42, 47, 66, 103,
    Haftar enrols, 47
Russia, 74

Sa'adi (tribes of Libya) 27, 28,
    44, 65, 95, 96, 112
Sadat, Anwar 32
Said, Ahmad, Egyptian
    propagandist, 50
Saif al-Nasr, Leading family of
    the Aulad Sulaim (Tribe) 27
Salafists, some notes on 152–153
Sarkozy, Nicholas, 134, and
    Bernard-Henri Lévy, 124–125,
    meets National Transition
    Councillor Mohammed Jebril,
    125, recognises the INC as

legitimate government of
Libya, 126
Sebha 27, 112
Senussi (Islamic Sufi sect) 25,
28, 41, 58, Mohamed ben
Ali al-Senussi 29, Sayyid
Idris al-Senussi 30, Emir Idris
al-Senussi and the Libyan
Arab Force 31, 36, 40, 56,
invited to take the throne of
Libya, 61, Idris al-Senussi
as King of Libya 41, Prince
Abdulla Abed aka the Black
Prince, 73, in Chad, 94
Senussi Arab Force 36
Seven Sisters, international oil
cartel, 74
Shaban, Omran, Misratan
militiaman, 139–140
Shelhi, Omar, favoured courtier
of King Idris, 67, 75
Shelhi, Azziz, Libyan Army Chief
of Staff for King Idris, 67
Shoura Council of Islamic Youth,
in Derna, 156–158
Sidra, oil terminal, 155
Sirte, Ghaddafi's birthplace, 43,
Ghaddadfa tribe's homeland,
43, Gaddafi at school in, 46,
Ghaddafi takes refuge in, 136,
Ghaddafi attempts to escape
and is killed, 136–137

Sirte, Gulf of (aka Sidra), 100,
US 6th Fleet enters, 100, Line
of Death, 100
Stevens, Christopher, US
Ambassador to Libya, death
in Benghazi 146–150
Stirling, David, Founder of the
SAS, 73
Sudan 35
Sudan Political Service, 58
Suez, Canal Zone, 51, 69

Tawergha, revenge attacks on by
Misratans, 132
Tebu 28, 29, 35, 65, background
58, 82–83, 94
Terbil, Fathi, human rights
lawyer, 117
Thuwwars (*see Militias*), and
larger formations defined,
133
Tibesti Mountains, 58, 82
Tobruk, 21, 28, 123, Royal
Palace 34
Toyota Wars (Chad), 84
Tripoli (Libya), 20, defeat of
Ghaddafi in, 134–136
Tripoli Military Council, 135,
139, 145
Tripolitania (see also West
Libya), 26, tribes of, 37

Tuareg and Tuaregs, 58, 65, 83, Ghaddafi's Tuareg mercenaries flee to Mali, 138

Turkey, 135

United Arab Emirates, 140

UN Commission for Human Rights, accuses some Misratan militias of torture, 145

United Nations, General Assembly, 59, 250th Plenary Meeting, 61

United Nations Security Council, voted in resolution 1973 which authorised a belligerent no-fly zone, 126

United States of America (USA), 59

USSR, 59, 77

UTA Flight, 772, 101

Voice of the Arabs radio station, 50, 64

Wadi Ben Jawad, 119

Wagner, Russian mercenaries, 35

Warfella (Tribe), 44, 76, 113, 136, 140

Western Mountains (*see Jebel Nefusa*)

Wright, John, on Ghaddafi's interventions in Chad, 81–82

Younis, Abul, 124, (*see al-Obeidi, Abdul Fatah Younis*)

Zaire (now the Democratic Republic of the Congo), 110

Zawiya (*aka Sway or Swai*) (Tribe) 23, 28, 29, 94, 154

Zawiyah, 135

Zidan, Ali, 147

Zintan, 35, 129, 134, 136, militias in Tripoli, 145

Ziou, Almahdi, role in revolt in Benghazi, 18